Putting the Pieces Together: Your Survival Guide to the First Five Years in Business

By Nicki Chang-Powless

PUTTING THE PIECES TOGETHER: Your Survival Guide to the First Five Years in Business

Copyright © 2018 to Nicki Chang-Powless

For more information, visit: www.NCPconsulting.net

Published by Heather Andrews @followitthrupublishing.com

www.heatherandrews.press

www.followitthrupublishing.com

Book cover design by Lorraine Shulba: www.bluebugstudios.com

Editing by Suzanne LaVoie: www.suzannelavoiewrites.com

Jen Sabillon: www.theladybosscollective.com

Copy editing manuscript compilation by Amanda: www.letsgetbooked.com

Formatting by Bojan Kratofil: www.expertformatting.com

ISBN: 978-1-5136-3987-1

ADVANCE PRAISE FOR

Putting the Pieces Together:
Your Survival Guide to the First Five Years in Business

"You can definitely see Nicki's business experience come out and shine in this book. She has a lot to offer as a business strategist, and this book captures the essence of the work she does. This guide to the first five years literally puts the pieces together for anyone starting out!"

- ILONA MAKAR, Owner CBWN, Connected Business Women Network Director Calgary Chapter

"This book captures the heart and anguish of the overwhelmed business owner. Simply putting together the pieces so they not only survive the first five years, but they thrive. A must read!"

DEBRA KASWOSKI, 3X Best-selling Author, Speaker, Executive Coach

"Nicki Chang-Powless' Survival Guide is a must-have for anyone starting a business. Nicki has been proven to be a 2nd to none business strategist for us at Jujube and to all of our members as well. She really knows how to take your business to the next level. This book answers a lot of the common questions and gives you the formula for success!"

CHRISTOPHER DARRYL, President of Jujube Business Builders

To my husband Ken who encouraged me to

"Fly, Little Birdie, Fly".

Thank you for all your support

and for giving me the strength to

Spread my wings and Fly!

ACKNOWLEDGEMENTS

As with any journey, whether it is business or personal, we are not alone. There is always a team of people behind the scenes putting everything in place and supporting us every step of the way.

I want to start off by thanking my amazing contributing experts who shared their expertise in this book. Together, we can help more new startup businesses gain the knowledge they need to succeed. A big thank you for your support in this project – Darlene Hull, Marion Skaja, Helene Wood, Todd Purcell, Heather Andrews, Tina Saini, Jennifer Belik, Lorraine Shulba and Catherine Saykaly-Stevens.

I am also grateful to Heather Andrews with Follow It Thru Publishing who helped me put all the pieces in place to publish my first book within the tight timeline I had set. Thank you to you and your team for doing an awesome job of coordinating everything and keeping everyone on track. You made everything very easy for me to follow, and it reduced my stress during the process.

Thank you Lorraine Shulba for creating a beautiful book cover that is able to portray the complexity of starting a business. I love how we were able to take this design concept and use it to brand the book in its promotion.

I want to also thank many of my colleagues for sharing their own publishing experience with me and guiding me through the process. Publishing my first book was a daunting task, and it was very comforting to know I was able to pick up the phone and get your perspective on a variety of topics.

Without the support of my family, friends, clients, acquaintances and business affiliates, I would not have had the courage to complete this book. Thank you for encouraging me to take this big step.

Most of all, I want to give a special thank you to my husband Ken Powless, my two girls, Alexis and Callie, and my mother for their endless support with my business and this book project. You put up with my endless questions to get a second opinion on a variety of topics, and I love you for it.

INTRODUCTION

It is alarming when I see the statistics that say only 50% of businesses will survive the first five years.

When I started my business in 2015, I was blown away when I realized that the business concepts and knowledge I had acquired over the past twenty-three years in the corporate world were not common knowledge within the startup community. This, unfortunately, explains those dismal failure statistics.

Through my experience of working with startup businesses, I found that many were not getting the results they had hoped for. I found the main reasons they were not succeeding were:

- They did not know what they did not know. There is so much to learn about business if you are not familiar with it. The amount of information out there is overwhelming, and business owners are having trouble processing what is required and when to incorporate the concepts.

- They did not have a clearly defined and validated plan to move forward. They would download a business plan template off the internet, fill it out, and voila! They had a business plan. Except, they really didn't have much of anything at all. They were missing the most important piece—the validation from experienced professionals that their plan had a strong chance for success along with the understanding of how to achieve their goals faster.

- They were taking steps for their business in the wrong order. Too many times, people spent money on something and did not get the desired results because they missed some crucial steps that needed to be done prior. As an example, if you spend money on an aggressive marketing campaign, but you do not have the infrastructure to properly handle the increased volume of business, then you could find yourself in trouble.

I wrote this book to give the startup community a guide to the many pieces that need to go together in order to achieve real, long-lasting results. This book is intended to summarize the different stages a business owner might endure in the first five years and to show them the steps required for true business success.

All businesses are different and will have unique needs. Not everything covered in this book will apply to everyone. It is intended to summarize all the different areas involved, and a general synopsis of what can happen should one follow the prescribed steps (without unforeseen circumstances, one simply cannot know in advance).

Each area on its own could potentially be its own book. My goal is merely to supply a checklist of items for you to be aware of and to investigate further should it apply to you. I also brought together some experts to share tips in their areas of specialty.

I tried to keep the principles covered in this book as generic as possible, so they may be applied internationally. As I am based in Canada, some of the principles may not apply if you are in a different country. It is always advisable to check on your legal responsibilities in your country/state of residence.

All content in this book is based on both my personal and corporate business experiences over a twenty-three year period in the oil and gas industry, as well as my work with startup businesses. My principles are based on common business practices.

I was very fortunate in my career to have had opportunities to experience all aspects of running a business, including strategic selling, marketing, software development, project management, personnel management, accounting, operations and eventually senior management. This allows me to specialize in giving business owners a holistic view of their businesses.

When I started my business in 2015, I was able to bring this knowledge to the startup industry. Two years later, I realized that the Kickstart Program I had developed was effective in helping overwhelmed business owners get clarity and direction. As the process got more refined, I was getting consistent results where people were getting their "AHA" moments at just about the same time in the process! Clients have described my process as life-changing, and that is exactly what my goal is each and every time.

I chose to write this book to give people the road map to achieve success. Now, it is in your hands. What you are about to experience will change your life if you let it. Are you ready?

Table of Contents

CHAPTER 1

WHAT TO EXPECT

There are many people who start a business. Everyone has their own reasons as to why they want to embark on the journey of entrepreneurship.

For many people, starting a business may mean taking a passion and monetizing it. Or it could be sharing your knowledge or skill to help others and to make the world a better place. It's about providing a product or service that people need.

On the personal side, one of the main reasons that people want to start a business is because they want flexible work hours. They may have a young family, so they want to be able to spend more time with them and to watch them grow up. Or maybe it's having the flexibility to do the things that they love to do. They want more spare time. This is one of the most common reasons why people begin an entrepreneurial path.

Another common reason is people want to be their own boss. Sometimes they have been disillusioned by working for a company that doesn't have the same values and ethics as they do. Or maybe their boss doesn't value them. Or perhaps the company is making decisions that they don't agree with. Many times, this is the motivating factor on why someone wants to start a business. They want to be able to call the shots and set the rules.

They may want to make more money. They don't want part of the money to go to someone else. They want to be able to control it.

These are some of the visions that motivate people to start a business. The reality is it takes time to build a business before you can see the benefits of owning one.

Are You Cut Out to be a Business Owner?

The most important quality or trait for a business owner is you should be able to take initiative and act on your ideas. It's fine to do a lot of planning and research, but the dream will never be a reality if you don't take the steps to move forward. As a business owner, you are the one responsible for creating the plan and executing it. You are your own boss, and there will be nobody to tell you what to do. It also means you are responsible to make sure the work is done properly, either by yourself or by someone else.

A business owner is usually a visionary that helps solve a problem in a unique way. It's providing a product or service and helping a community. You want to make an impact on other people's lives while trying to solve their problems.

In terms of personality, you should be a people person and a good communicator. There is a heavy social component to the sales and marketing side. Even if you hire somebody to do the sales, you should still have good people skills to deal with your team. You want to be able to motivate your team, so they perform to the best of their ability, without having to rule by fear. You will need to be able to wear your psychologist hat in this function.

It also helps if you are organized. If you are not naturally organized, then you should consider working with someone who is— either a business partner or a hired assistant. There are a lot of things that you need to be accountable for, including reporting to government agencies, and if you ever go public, accountable to your shareholders.

One important thing to keep in mind is that not everyone is made to be an entrepreneur and that's okay. If you are having doubts, consider interviewing a few entrepreneurs and if they don't mind, maybe job shadow them. This will give you a taste of whether this is right life for you.

> *Running a business takes a lot of time and effort. It also requires a lot of focus to stay on track.*

Work-Life Balance

One of the biggest sacrifices that people make is in the work-life balance. Owning a business will have a huge impact on your life. It's not an easy thing to do to start a business. It takes a lot of time and commitment.

The one thing that gets sacrificed is family time. If your clients have a specific request and there is a deadline to meet, then it needs to get done. Many people start out as a solopreneur. This means you are the only one running the show. If you have a deadline, then you need to decide whether work will take priority over your family. The reason being that your family income contribution might be dependent on the success of your business. This is especially important if you are the sole breadwinner in the household.

Running a business takes a lot of time and effort. It also requires a lot of focus to stay on track. If you are in an environment where there is a young child that constantly needs your attention, this can impact how much work gets done.

Raising a family may be your priority. You should understand that the expectations you put on your business will be impacted by your family commitment. Depending on how fast you want your business to grow, sometimes sacrifices will need to be made. If you want your business to be successful faster, you may need to put that family vacation on hold while you are in the process of getting the business off the ground. The more time you spend on the business, the faster you will be able to achieve your goals.

You may not want your family life to be affected by having a business. The reality is your customers may dictate how you spend your time. They are the ones who are putting the food on your table, and they are the real boss. It is important to be able to set the proper expectations with your customers upfront and come up with a proper balance. Communication will be key. Perhaps you only take appointments until 3 PM so you can pick up the kids from school. Or Sunday is your family day, and everyone knows it.

There will be struggles trying to balance time commitments. Your customers will have some control over your schedule. Keep in mind that customer appointments bring in revenue and personal time does not. This is a reality.

There will be times where you may need to miss family commitments because of a work priority. Sometimes the family schedule can become distracting when you are working on a big project for your business.

Even being sick can have an impact on your business. When I suddenly had my appendix removed, I had to cancel all my appointments for the day and reschedule everything. It also meant not getting paid for the work I didn't do. As an employee of a company, you have the luxury of getting paid sick days. As a business owner, if you are not working, the money will not be coming in when you are still in startup mode.

Once your business is more established, the situation may change and the rewards will follow. Unfortunately, it takes a lot of blood, sweat, tears and sacrifices to get to that point.

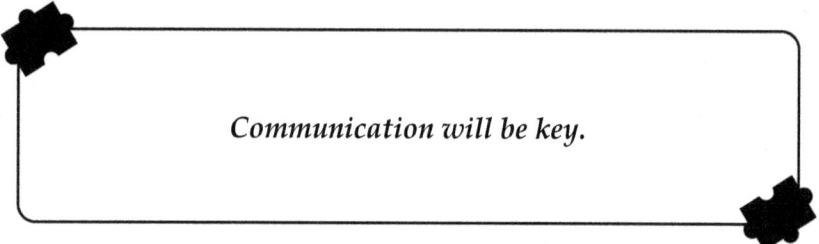

Communication will be key.

How Much Money Do You Need to Get Started?

Money is a huge topic when starting a business. It's difficult to answer the question of how much you need to get started, as it really depends on the type of business you are getting into. Does your business require that you purchase equipment, or enter into a lease agreement? If you provide a service, it is quite possible that all you need is a computer and an office in your home. In this case, you don't need a lot of money to get started.

Understanding the amount of money needed to survive the startup period is more important than knowing how much money you need to get started. When you first open the doors to your business, people won't just start coming in right away to buy your product or service. It takes time to get the word out to people. This means you need to survive the initial startup period as you still need to put food on the table and pay your bills.

If you are going to be using money from savings, you should put together a budget that shows how much you normally spend in one week or one month including the everyday expenses of both your personal and business life. This will give you an idea of how long you have before the money runs out. You need to also take into account unemployment payments or any other income that is coming in. This will help in the planning stage.

Balancing a Job and Business

Many people keep their full-time jobs until their business gets up and going. The reality is, if you are working a forty hour per week job, there is little time and energy left to also work on a business full-time on the side. If you have a young family, there is even less time to devote to building a business.

The time factor is only one thing. There is also your energy level. You should have some downtime and self-care to be able to continually motivate yourself to work on your new business and your current job. The reality is you should invest full-time hours on your business to move ahead quickly. You cannot expect to get a forty hours per week results while only putting in ten hours per week. This is not realistic. There are many people who eventually quit their full-time job to pursue their dream of owning their own business.

A part-time job makes more logical sense. It allows you to have some income while you are trying to build your business. It is a good idea to track the hours that you are working on your business. It will give you some idea as to whether you were putting in the time commitment required to achieve your goals. A standard work week is forty hours per week. However, many business owners work more than this if they want to see results sooner.

> *You cannot expect to get a forty hours per week results while only putting in ten hours per week.*

If you have a job and you own your own home, you should consider taking out a line of credit on your home while you are still employed. Banks are more likely to approve the line of credit when you have full-time employment. It is not the intention to use the line of credit for your business. Rather, it is good to have the line of credit in case of an emergency when you are not employed and need the extra money during the startup phase of your business. Having a higher credit card limit is also helpful. Keep in mind, it is not the intention to use up the credit card and line of credit limits. It is only there for you in case of an emergency. You should avoid using the credit lines and increasing your debt if you can.

Another reality for a business owner is that it may be tricky to get a mortgage. You don't have the guaranteed income that employees do, so lending institutions may be hesitant to loan you the money to buy a house. If your business is new, you may not have the track record to show the income coming in. Ideally, it's good to have your mortgage situation in place before you start a business. There are professional mortgage brokers who may be able to help business owners get approved for a mortgage, as it is not a simple process.

Life Cycle of a Startup Business

A business typically goes through a number of stages. The following describes what you might be able to expect with your business when you start.

The first phase of a business is sales and marketing. Without any sales, you don't really have a business. You are pounding the pavement trying to get the word out. You are in the process of building your credibility and your reputation.

Once people start getting to know who you are, and you are gaining momentum in your sales, there will come a time when you will realize that you can't keep up with the work, and you're starting to pull your hair out! It could be with the follow-up to your clients, or trying to keep the administrative stuff in place to run your business. Regardless, you have entered into the next stage of the business.

At this second stage, you are now focusing on building your team, building systems to make things run smoother, and possibly incorporating a level of automation into your processes. You are not a one-person operation anymore. Congratulations—you have outgrown this!

Once you have completed the first two stages, then you can actually focus on making your business more profitable. Up until now, the money you are making might be reinvested into the business to automate it, or used to hire contractors to help you over the hump. In this third phase, you are looking at other ways to make more profit. It is usually at this stage when the money starts rolling in and you can relax a bit in your business.

The fourth and final stage is growth. This is when you can start looking at targeting new industries or adding new products. At this stage, you are actually going right back to the beginning again except, this time around, it will go much faster, as most of your systems are already in place, and you are more experienced in the process.

Depending on the type of industry you are in and how unique your product and service is, the entire cycle can vary in time. There are owners that have been in business for over 10 years that are still in the second stage. They still don't have efficient systems in place, so their growth and their income potential are capped. They cannot take vacation without their business coming to a standstill.

On the other end of the spectrum, some businesses grow too fast. The product or service is unique, and there is a lot of interest in it. They become profitable very quickly. The dilemma they run into is that they may not be able to keep up with the demand of the product as they may not have been able to put the systems in place to sustain the growth. . These can be huge problems to have and may also be the downfall of the business.

What to know about business

There is a lot to learn about running a successful business. It is not necessary to know everything upfront. It's a matter of taking the initiative to learn what you may not know. Reading this book is definitely a great first step.

Usually in the larger cities, you will find many free educational events to support startup businesses. Some are government initiatives. It's a matter of finding out what is happening in your community. There are also networking events that will combine business education as part of their program. This way you can make new contacts while learning some of the fundamentals of business. Additionally, there are courses and programs available to help you gain the business knowledge you need to run a successful business. Some are even offered online, so you can go through them at your leisure.

One word of caution when embarking on your educational journey; many people find the quantity of information overwhelming. Part of it is because some of the knowledge may not be relevant at your stage of the business. This can make things very confusing.

Everything you are learning about sales, marketing and business, can be viewed as tools in your toolbox. You are learning how to use the power saw, hammer, and screwdriver. The challenge is understanding when to use the specific tool under what circumstance.

If you are trying to build a house, you need to know what the house looks like first. This is your vision for the company. In order to build the house, you need to have a set of blueprints. These blueprints will tell you that the plumbing needs to go in before the walls go up. It tells you what order things should be put in place by when. It is this blueprint that will tell you which tools to use at what time. This applies to business too – you need a blueprint to guide you.

You may choose to work with a business professional to help guide you on this journey. They will make the journey move faster, as you won't need to learn things the hard way or reinvent the wheel. These professionals can be in the form of a coach, strategist, mentor or adviser. It is not necessary to reinvent the wheel and it's good to get a set of outside eyes to look at your situation.

When looking for someone to work with, please keep in mind that there are many areas of specialty in business. Some people may be strong on the sales and marketing side, but may not be strong on the operations or financial side. It is important to understand who you are working with and their strengths.

During an athlete's career, they may go through a number of different coaches. The gym teacher in elementary school may have been the one who showed them the basic skills. As they advanced to university level, their coaches might be more competitive. If one day this athlete decided to go for the gold at the Olympics, they would most likely align themselves with an Olympic level coach. On the Olympics side, they would most likely have coaches for different areas. They would have one specifically helping them with their technique and skills of the sport. They may also have coaches on the sideline that deal with nutrition, injury prevention, performance, mindset and other areas.

It's the same thing in business. It's a matter of finding the right person to help you with the different stages of your business. The person that helps you start up may not be the same person to help you take your company public. You should also find someone that aligns with your core values and your personality.

The most important thing when embarking on this educational journey is to ask a lot of questions. If you don't understand something, get clarification. If someone is not taking the time to explain things to you, then they might not be the right person for you to work with. Also, you will find that different people will have different opinions on the same topic. It's a matter of understanding how it might impact your specific business and what is right for you. Furthermore, diverse people have various personalities and styles. Choose the one that works best with you.

You should recognize that you are not alone on this journey. If you align yourself with the right people, you will be able to reach your destination much faster. In this collaborative process, you should be open to new ideas. Sometimes the most obscure suggestions can turn into something very profitable.

CHAPTER 2

GETTING STARTED

You are ready and committed to taking that first step forward. Now what?

Let's begin by seeing if you actually have a viable business idea and how to get started if you do.

Keep in mind that not all ideas are successful at the starting gate or hit the nail on the head to begin with. Many ideas start with one thing in mind and evolve over time to become stronger.

Testing the Market

To give yourself the best chance of getting the business thing right from the start, you should begin by doing some research.

There are many people in the world who come up with these really awesome and interesting ideas. They go full steam ahead realizing that, even though it sounds interesting, people just won't commit to buying it. Or they stumble (or fall flat on their faces) upon the fact that the cost to create the product is too high for what the market is willing to pay for it.

You need to get these answers *before* you invest too much of your own time and money into your idea.

Start by deciding who your target market is and how large that market truly is.

I originally wanted to start a business helping high net worth working professionals incorporate a strategy to build their retirement portfolio rather than a cash flow stream.

What I quickly realized was that the number of people who would be interested in this strategy was a very small niche market. I also realized that the economy was not ideal for this service at the time. After doing this much-needed research, I abandoned the idea and went in a different direction. This was a great decision, but one I would not have made had I not done the research first.

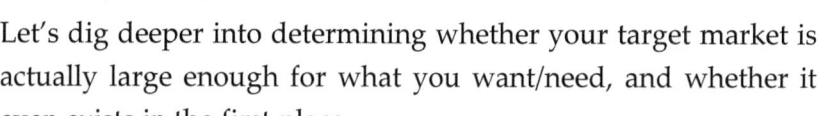

Start by deciding who your target market is and how large that market truly is.

Let's dig deeper into determining whether your target market is actually large enough for what you want/need, and whether it even exists in the first place.

Step one - To determine the size of a market, you can use databases to get relevant statistics. Don't let this strategy overwhelm you, because it really is a simple process.

Since there are many ways to conduct a study under many different parameters, you ideally should get validation of your numbers from multiple sources, especially if you are using the internet for your research.

Your public library is also a great source of information. Librarians are trained to know how to get the information you need. Some libraries also have access to paid databases so you can expand your search. All of these information sources are great for getting you the answers you need when you need them.

Step two – You need to see if there is actually any interest in your idea. The best way to do this is to simply *ask*. The important thing to remember here is: don't just ask anyone. Make sure to ask your *target market*. Knowing who your target market (who you want to serve with your products or services) is crucial to this step.

For a business that produces a consumer-based product, I have seen people simply conduct a survey at the local shopping mall. Come up with easy questions for them to answer, and conduct the survey right there in the middle of the mall to your *target market*.

Step three – If you are getting interest in your product or service, the next logical question is, "How much would you pay for this product or service?"

When you ask this question, don't put a number into their mind. Just pause and let them think about it. This is a sure way for you to find out what it is really worth to them. You should also see a pattern emerge from the answers.

Keep in mind that the price people are willing to pay may vary greatly. If there is a large discrepancy of what some would pay versus others, then perhaps what you presented is too broad. Some people might be thinking something *big* and some might think it's *small*. If this happens, you will definitely need to revisit your scope.

Step four – Now that you have a good idea of what people are willing to pay for your product/service, you need to figure out your costs, and whether you can produce and deliver the product at a cost that will still allow you to make money in the process.

You should not only include the costs to buy your materials, but also your time to put it together, cost of goods, and your overhead to own a company. Your overhead is the cost to run your business regardless of whether you have customers or not. If you have no customers, you still need to pay items like your rent, utilities, insurance, advertising, etc. These costs would be considered your overhead.

Sometimes, the results of this exercise say you cannot make money at all with what you want to do/produce. Word to the wise: don't let this discourage you! Sometimes it's a matter of fine tuning your product or service offering in a specific manner so you *can have a profitable business*.

Other Business Opportunities

Not all businesses are based on you bringing a new idea to market. Here are some other ways you can get into the business world:

- Buy into a franchise.
- Buy an existing business.
- Enter into a partnership agreement with an existing business.

No matter which direction you decide to go in, it is important to get a professional evaluation done by a qualified accountant before taking a leap. Note that your tax accountant may not be qualified to help you in this area, as it is its own specialty in accounting. If you need help finding a qualified accountant to help value a business, consult with another business owner, get a referral from your tax accountant, or do your research via the internet.

You should also hire a lawyer to review the terms of the business agreement. The lawyer you hire will look after your best interests and not of the interest of the other person. You should never save costs to have one lawyer look at both sides of the transaction. This can create a messy situation that could possibly hinder you in the longer run.

Depending on what business you are getting involved in, you should approach it with caution and due diligence.

Do your homework! Talk to references and experts involved in the industry. Ask them if the business has a culture and core values that you can easily integrate into? Why are they selling in the first place? It's more work up front, but it will give you a complete picture of what you are getting into.

> *Word to the wise: don't let this discourage you! Sometimes it's a matter of fine tuning your product or service offering in a specific manner so you can have a profitable business.*

Business vs Practice

For people getting into a service related business like a health practitioner, you need to ask yourself whether you are building a business or a practice. The approach you take with one type of business is different than with the other type.

So, what is the difference?

Opening a practice would mean you are not only running the business; you are also delivering the service.

Massage therapists or consultants are perfect examples of a practice. These people are the equivalent of being an employee of a company, except they can set their own hours, control the numbers of clients they have, and they decide how much to charge for their services.

On the flip side, they are also responsible for looking for their own clients and the administration of running a business.

The key thing about a practice is there are only so many hours in a day that you can be servicing clients. This means your income is capped at the number of hours you can work. Also, if you are not working or on vacation, then there is no money coming into the business at all.

A business, on the other hand, is structured so that if the owner goes on vacation, the business is still operating normally and bringing in income.

In the example of the massage therapist, a massage therapy business would have a number of massage therapists working under the main company. A business would take a product or service that is scalable and expands it into a larger scope.

Another example of a business could be offering online courses where people simply download the material from the internet. You do not have to be there for them to take the course. It is an automated process which brings in passive income (income that comes in without one-to-one interaction with clients or customers).

If you are a service-based business, it's possible you may start off as a practice to learn the ropes, get experience, and put things in place for growth. Eventually, though, you can grow to become a business.

Building a practice and building a business both require different growth strategies. A business has the potential for creating and building greatness.

The Company Name

Now that you know what type of business you want to start, *and* you have done preliminary research, you are now ready to launch.

However, you can't launch a company without a company name!

This is the fun part!

Picking a company name can be really stressful. Sometimes we try too hard and nothing jumps out at us at the start. If you have patience, the name will eventually come to you.

Some people come up with really interesting names that mean something personally to them. Some people have even used mind mapping exercises to come up with their name.

If coming up with a name is not working for you, there are a number of free random name generator apps online to help the creative juices get flowing. Some companies just use the owner's initials, or when you are really drawing a complete blank, you can just use the next sequence in the government database and register as a numbered company.

Ideally, your full company name should include what you do as a product or service. For example, I did not want to delay the launch of my business and could not come up with a good company name. So, I decided to just use my initials and call it **NCP Consulting Services**. If I come up with a better name in the future, I will consider paying to have it changed through the appropriate government channels.

Here are some tips to consider when picking a name:

- Search the internet to see what others are using and what is already taken (this can help you avoid legal battles, wasting money on branding that won't work, etc.).

- Search the internet to see if there are other businesses in other industries associated with the same name. Look not only on the local level, but also on a global level to ensure you're covering all your bases.

- Can your potential company name be shortened into an acronym? If so, is it similar to someone else's company name? Or does the acronym have a negative image associated with it? Neither of these situations are ideal.

When you actually go to register your company's name, there will most likely be a name search that will be done. It will show what other company names are similar to yours.

Company Structures

There are a number of different ways you can structure your business. Different regions and countries may have different terminology, but the principles should all be similar.

Being a sole proprietor is the most common place to start. It is usually for people with a business that does not have a high level of business liability. Being a sole proprietor means you do not have legal liability coverage in case someone wanted to pursue a lawsuit against your company.

If you are in a high-risk industry, such as taking people skydiving, you would probably want to incorporate your business from the beginning. Incorporating your business means that you are taking the necessary legal steps to cover your business from any legal action that may take place and leave you with limited personal responsibility (which can affect your entire life such as finances, home, etc.).

Becoming an incorporated business should limit your liability and protect your personal assets. The cost to incorporate your business will typically be higher than acting as a sole proprietor.

You should consult with a business lawyer to see what is best suited for your situation. You can always start as a sole proprietor and incorporate later, once you are more established.

If you decide to form a partnership with one or more individuals, there are more things to consider.

It's really nice to be able to work in a team environment from the start. After all, two heads are better than one, right? However, here are things to consider when going into a partnership:

- **Personality fit** – look at how well you get along with each other. Don't go into the relationship in anticipation that the person will change. Chances are they will not change. Sometimes that gut feeling is enough to go on. If it doesn't feel right, then it probably isn't.

- **Core values** – it is important to have your core values in alignment. Do you both value customer service and the pursuit of excellence, or does one like to cut corners and produce cheap quality goods? Knowing this before you commit can be a lifesaver in the long run.

- **Previous relationship** – starting a business with your best friend since high school or relative can mean that your personal relationship may impact how you make business decisions as you risk possibly hurting the other person's feelings. You not only risk losing the business, but potentially a friendship too.

When the tough decision of parting ways needs to be made, you must remember that this is *business* and *not personal*.

- **Length of relationship** - Some people go into a partnership with someone they don't know very well. This is risky, too. It's like getting married after only dating for 6 months. Everything is still very fresh and exciting when you are starting out. Then, the true personalities come out.

- **Skills** - evaluate what skills everyone brings to the table. You want the skill sets to be complementary so that it's well-defined as to who is taking on what role. Being a responsible business owner means one of you needs to be organized and build in a level of accountability for government and financial reporting, while the other partner may be the sales and marketing person.

- **Weathering the financial storm** – there are always financial storm that comes with all startups. We all go into a partnership with a level of optimism. The real question is can you both afford to contribute to the company when things are not going as planned?

- **Exit strategy** – The exit is not always about people not getting along or the business not doing well. Sometimes it's because one person's life direction has changed, and they want to do something else. It's important to have this discussion up front so the exit strategy and terms are properly defined without having tempers flared and people not thinking rationally.

With all business agreements, it is recommended to have lawyers involved. Notice this is in the plural form. You do not want to get one lawyer to draw up the agreement for the both of you. You want a lawyer who will look after *your* best interests and not that of the group. Making the investment up front, such as signing a prenup before your wedding, will be worth it in the end.

Once you know what corporate structure you want in place, it's time to register your business. There are usually different sets of rules for the city, province/state, and country you live in. It is your responsibility to know what the proper rules are at your location and adhere to them.

Living only a few hours away from beautiful Banff National Park, many people don't know that wedding photographers in Banff must register themselves with the townsite, or they risk being fined. They also may not know that there are safety regulations about where you can fly a drone, and that it is disallowed in a national park.

Many cities also require that you apply for a business license to work from your home as neighbors may complain about increased traffic to the street and the reduced number of parking spaces.

Another thing you should know is what the taxation requirements are for the area you are operating from; you may need to collect taxes and remit them to the proper government agencies. Failure to do so in a timely manner can mean fines.

Also, if you are in one location and your client is in another, you may wonder what taxes you should charge. Consult a tax accountant to make sure you are doing things properly, as it could cost you major penalties if you don't do it right.

Business Address

It is a trend for people to now work from home. You can save money by not paying rent to someone else, and your travel time is reduced to just walking downstairs to your office. This situation is not for everyone.

It requires discipline to not get distracted by the dirty dishes in the sink or a program on TV when you should be working.

It can also get lonely as the social interaction is reduced.

If you decide to work from home, there are a few things to consider:

- Do you want your home address posted as your place of business? You lose your privacy, and it may be perceived as a small business. You can rent a post office box nearby to give the perception of a commercial business address. You just have to remember to pick up your mail!

- You should notify your home insurance carrier to let them know you have a home office. If you have inventory in your business and something happens, your insurance company may not cover you if they don't know about your business. Your insurance company may also cover any equipment you have that is related to your business—like a photographer's camera gear or a laptop that gets stolen.

- Track your home receipts like utilities as you might be able to claim some of it as a business expense. This is usually based on a percentage of your home that is being used for business. Talk to your tax accountant to find out what receipts you should be tracking.

For those who have too many distractions at home, lack discipline, or prefer to work outside, there are office spaces you can rent. If you don't need something full-time, co-working spaces may be available in your area where you can rent an office for so many days per month. This allows you to get out of the house, make connections, and only pay for what you use.

Before you sign a lease to rent space, keep in mind that this is an additional expense for your business. As a startup, you might not be able to afford the rent. Or you might find better places to spend your money to help with the startup phase—like advertising.

Once you sign a contract, you are committed to paying this expense regardless of whether you have clients or not.

Another cost-effective option is to work out of a public library or have meetings in coffee shops or at your client's office.

Basic Systems to Set Up a Business

To be a successful business, you need to build systems for your business to run smoothly. During the startup phase, this does not need to be elaborate. Here is a checklist of some of the basic things you need in place from the start:

Invoicing and collections system – Congratulations, you just made your first sale! Now what? You need to bill the client, so you can collect money! Then, you can celebrate your FIRST sale!

There are many different systems to help you invoice and collect payments from clients/customers. Choosing the right system really depends on the type of business you have.

Let's start with a business that will be invoicing or billing for services. This is where you send the invoice and allow your client to pay at a later date.

In these situations, you can either manually create invoices or look at one of the many different invoicing systems available. It's a matter of finding one that you feel most comfortable with. Some have fees, and some can integrate with your accounting system.

If you have an accountant, they can help guide you in your selection. If you don't have an accountant, there are many software programs that offer a free trial period. Download one to see how you like it. If you don't like it, remember to cancel your subscription or they will start charging you after the free trial runs out.

Once you have sent out the invoice to your client, you still have to collect payment. To save on fees, some businesses will only accept cash, cheque or e-transfer. However, this may not be convenient for everyone. The world of credit cards opens the door to many more options and decisions to be made.

If your business requires payments right away, such as retail or online stores, you will need to find a system that works best for your product or service. When you go to the bank to open a standard business account, some banks will ask whether you want to be set up to accept credit cards for payment. They will typically refer you to their partnered payment processor. Since there are many programs out there, you should consider shopping around before committing and investing.

When looking to accept credit card payments, here are some things you should know before you start your research. The solution that is right for you will depend on how you answer these questions:

- Will the credit card be present during the transaction, or are you manually entering their credit card information into the system?

- What is the estimated amount of credit card transactions per month and the volume? Take your best guess based on your average sale total per transaction and the number of transactions you expect per month. Also, how many are estimated to have the card present and how many without?

- Will there be recurring payments where the same amount is charged every month, as in a monthly subscription?

- Do you need to store credit card information for repetitive payments, where the amount of each transaction will vary? Keep in mind that you are responsible for keeping your customers' credit card information secure and will need an encrypted solution that is PCI certified and built specifically for this purpose. If any of your customers are in the EU, you will also need to be GDPR compliant.

- Do you want the credit card system to integrate with specific software, like accounting or point of sales software?

Jennifer Belik, of KIS Payments, helps people with their credit card needs. She explains that when it comes to transaction fees, there are different pricing structures, and not all of them may be offered up front. "No pricing structure is inherently 'bad'. You will want to be sure you understand how the pricing structure being offered will affect the 'bottom line' of your processing costs based on your actual sales transactions."

- **Flat rate** – This is easiest to understand and reconcile. All transactions are processed at one set rate. This is rarely the lowest rate.

- **Discount/Tiered** – You are charged a specified rate on the entire processing volume, plus additional tiered rates. This can be the trickiest to determine the bottom line cost of a transaction.

- **Interchange plus/"Cost plus"** – This is the most transparent and accountable option which discloses the exact costs related to your processing volume and the profit margin the processor earns on your account.

Your total transaction fee will be comprised of three components – the interchange fee which goes to the bank that issued the card, the assessment fee that goes to the card brand, and the processor's fee.

"Before making a decision, you will want to make sure you understand the 'whole package' you are selecting," states Jennifer Belik.

According to Jennifer, "One of the easiest mistakes to fall into when you are comparing payment solutions is to focus on one number or rate and assume that the 'lowest bidder' is your best option."

Jennifer further explains, "When you have problems with anything related to your credit card service, it can give you peace of mind to have a representative to help you investigate the situation and be your advocate with the processing platform. Make sure you understand what support is available to you after you have signed the contract. Will you have a personalized direct support person or a 1-800 number?"

Download your guide on what to consider when selecting a processing provider at www.kispayments.com/5YearBizGuide

Jennifer Belik suggests that you "take the time to talk to someone who can explain the options and help you select the right solution for you. Like us as individuals, no two businesses are exactly the same. Every scenario is going to be different."

Tracking expenses – It is extremely important to know what you are spending on your business. All of those expenses you have for your business are tax deductible and may count as write offs against your income.

If you make $50,000 in a year, the government will collect taxes based on this $50,000.

If you spend $20,000 running your business, then you can deduct $20,000 from your $50,000 income. This means you will pay taxes on $30,000 instead of the original $50,000. Wouldn't you rather pay less taxes? Talk to your local tax accountant to find out what your eligible write off expenses are. Bottom line: keep all of your receipts associated with your business.

If you keep losing your receipts, you need to come up with a system that ensures you will not lose them as they are worth money! There are some accounting programs that allow you to take a picture of the receipt right there on the spot. Or maybe you'll put an envelope in the spot that you normally take out your wallet to remind yourself to stash the receipts right away.

Another business expense you can claim is the mileage on your car. If you have a car that is used exclusively for business, then you just need to save the receipts associated with the vehicle, like fuel, service maintenance, insurance, and registration.

However, if you use your car for both business and personal usage, you need to track your mileage. The percentage you use for business can be claimed. This may also help reduce the amount of business taxes you pay at the end of the year.

The tricky part here is to remember to track your mileage. There are applications you can download onto your phone to help with tracking. Or you can calculate mileage once a week, or even once a month, based on what you record on your calendar and calculate the distance using a mapping program. Regardless of what system you use, the trick is to get into the habit of doing it. If you find one system is not working for you, then change it. Keep changing it until you find one that *does* work. You don't want to be throwing money away if you can help it.

Bank account – It is always a good idea to get a separate bank account that is dedicated strictly to your business transactions. Your bookkeeper or accountant will be very happy to find that your business and personal transactions are not mixed. They won't have to spend time trying to figure out what is relevant to your business or not. Headache saved for all!

For convenience, it's nice to have your business bank account at the same bank as your personal one. This way you can start building a relationship with the bank. This may come in handy if you ever need financing for your business.

Technology – We live in a digital age. Everything we do seems to live on our computer or portable devices. Privacy and confidentiality need to be taken very seriously.

The reality is that there are malicious people out there in the world that may try to hack your computer or hold your data for ransom. It is very important to invest in good software protection and to have a good back-up strategy. If this is not your comfort zone, you should consider hiring someone who can help you design the workflows you need to minimize interruption to your business. Unfortunately, I have had viruses on my computer in the past, and each time it took several days for me to recover from the ugly situation.

To avoid this from happening, ensure that your passwords are strong, don't click on links from unfamiliar sources and keep your virus protection software up-to-date at all times!

Paying someone to take care of your computer properly is worth the investment to prevent future headaches. With technology these days, there are some systems that allow support businesses to log onto your computer remotely and support you that way. You can save yourself the transportation fee associated with them coming to you.

Insurance

You work hard to build your business, so make sure that you protect what you've built. The insurance world can be complicated at times. There are different policies for different situations. Helene Wood, an insurance professional with Advance Insurance, wants to share the most common concepts that apply to a business when it comes to insurance.

"Your broker is there to protect you and your business. Work closely with them and disclose your entire situation so they can make sure you have the proper coverage. If your situation changes, let your broker know. If you don't, you risk that your claim will not be covered, and you will be personally liable for damages," says Helene.

Home office insurance – This insurance is usually an add-on to your existing home insurance policy. This insurance gives you permission to run a business from your home. It protects your business equipment, like computers, against theft and damage. It also gives you protection if a client injures themselves coming to visit you at your home office. If you don't disclose that you have a business in your home and there is a claim, the insurance company can deny the entire claim.

Vehicle insurance for business – The insurance company needs to be aware that you are using your vehicle for business purposes.

The first step is to determine whether you are carrying commercial products in your vehicle - such as the inventory that you sell.

If you do, it is possible that your vehicle is now being used for commercial use. A commercial policy is different than a business one. If you get into an accident carrying commercial products under a business policy, you risk having your claim denied. This includes damages to your own vehicle and other vehicles affected in the accident.

Choose wisely. It is your business...protect it!

Business insurance – Depending on the type of business you are in, there are different types of business insurance coverages. Business insurance typically covers small businesses, whereas commercial insurance will cover a larger organization with many employees that have business facilities, including offices, warehouse, manufacturing plant, retail store, etc.

For business insurance, here is a list of what can be impacted:

- **Commercial general liability** - This coverage protects against injury or damages from people who attend your workshop or event. If you are renting or leasing an office or venue, many landlords will not cover this under their own insurance.

- **Special event insurance** - This insurance covers you for injuries if things get out of hand at an event, whether there is alcohol or not. You may still be liable if the person leaves the event and causes injury or damages due to consuming alcohol at your event.

- **Error and Omissions** - This coverage protects you in case you unintentionally give someone bad professional advice. If you are selling services into a different country, then your insurance company needs to know this information, as the rules may be different in other countries.

- **Inventory** - This type of insurance covers your commercial products against loss.

- **Business interruption** - With this insurance, you will be covered if you are unable to run your business for a period of time (for example, if a fire that breaks out at your warehouse).

- **Cyber** - This will help you recover from your systems being hacked, theft of private information, or having your data held hostage, should that situation arise. The selling of goods online would also be covered under cyber, along with the receiving of unwanted viruses during the transfer of data between computers. Cyber will protect you more completely against the digital world.

- **Directors and officers insurance** - This coverage protects the personal assets of the directors, officers, and their spouses against any lawsuits related to wrongful acts, such as wrongful dismissal, employee abuse, breach of fiduciary duty, and/or the board's failure to properly disburse funds (i.e. insurance proceeds).

Commercial insurance policies can get complicated. Here are some of the things the policies could be looking at:

- **Product liability** - If you are a manufacturer of product, you must be aware of any damage/injury your product may have caused. Also, if your product needs to be recalled for any reason, the only way you will be protected from this loss is if you have a policy that covers this possibility.

- **Shipping** - If you are shipping your goods outside of your home country, then you need to ensure you have the proper coverage in place.

- **Safety** - For injuries, the burden of proof is on the company to show they did their due diligence and have the appropriate policies and procedures in place to ensure a safe environment for employees and visitors. For example, mopping up spills when they occur and putting up a sign to show that the floor is wet, so people don't slip is a great example of a company doing their due diligence. If the company does not do this, it can be considered "contributory negligence" and can affect how much the insurance company pays out. You might have to take on a portion of the loss if you can't prove that you did your due diligence.

Please note that intentional and criminal acts are not covered by any insurance policy, as these acts typically fall under the criminal act.

**Download your list of things to bring
when getting commercial insurance at
www.aieacademy.ca/5YearBizGuide**

Helene Wood warns, "When choosing an insurance professional, be selective. Choose someone that you like and trust. Don't look at insurance as a necessary evil. Look at it and your insurance professional as being a strong strategic partner who is there to protect all that you have worked for to get where you are now and beyond."

Trust is the most important component in this partnership. Find that person, choose that person, and work closely with that person. Remember that your insurer is doing what they are doing so that you can do what you are doing. Without them, you truly would not be able to be in business.

Choose wisely. It is your business…protect it!

When looking at personal insurance, you also need to consider the following insurances:

Disability and critical illness insurance – If you and your business brings in your sole family income, you should consider disability and critical illness insurance. How are you going to pay your rent and bills if you are in an accident or you go in for surgery and cannot work? This type of insurance can help cover those times when unforeseen circumstances arise.

This type of insurance coverage is also good to have on key personnel in your organization. How will the company run if these people are suddenly affected by illness or an accident?

Life insurance - If you have a business partnership or a group of senior executives that run your business, it is a good idea to also consider life insurance on these people. If one person dies, how will this impact your operations? Life insurance will help alleviate the burden on the business.

Service Agreement

In the beginning stages of business, we all tend to be very trusting that our clients will pay us, or that the supplier will deliver what they promise. The reality is people can be forgetful or remember things differently. This is why it's a good idea to record things in writing so that everyone is on the same page in regard to what is supposed to be delivered and at what price.

Instead of doing business on a hand shake, at a bare minimum, it should be recorded in an email or text that you can refer back to.

However, as you become more accomplished and have experienced too many "misunderstandings", you will begin to see the value of creating a formal document outlining the details of your service and expectations. This comes with skillset and knowledge, as you begin to offer consistent services to your clients.

The higher the liability associated with your business, the more you should consider getting a lawyer to review your situation to help you draw up proper documents that are customized to your business.

It might be confidentiality clauses, protecting your intellectual property, or waivers explaining the risks involved with a certain activity. Having a lawyer look these over will be worth the investment in the long run. Trust me.

Once you have the text for the document the way you like it, here are some good common best practices for contracts:

- If your document is more than one page, put page 1 of XX (total number) pages on each sheet. In case someone prints the document, they will know if they are missing a page.

- Put your company name and contact information on each page.

- Always send the document in PDF format so the recipient cannot change something in the middle of the document without you knowing about it.

Professionals to Consult

We covered a lot of things to put in place when you start a business. Some of you can do it yourself, and some will require help from a professional. Either way, it's okay. No one starts a business knowing exactly what they need to do.

If you find yourself needing to consult with a professional for any reason, the following are key people that can help you over the startup hump:

- **Tax Accountant** – They will show you how to reduce your taxes.

- **Lawyer** – Make sure you and your company are protected at all times.

- **Information Systems** – Protect your data and computer systems.

- **Business Professional** – These people will help guide you on your business journey, so you can accelerate your results by leveraging off of their experience.

Keep in mind that you are in business to produce a product or service. You should *not* spend your time trying to be an expert in any of the above-mentioned areas (unless your business is one of these areas!).

Your time is better spent promoting *your* business. You do, however, need to know the basics in each area so you can make.

On your road trip, you may run into unexpected detours and construction zones.

CHAPTER 3

THE BUSINESS PLAN

Many successful business people will say the key to a starting a business is to have a solid plan. This is true, to some extent, but only if you have enough business experience to know what you are doing and to know what makes sense to put into the plan.

There are many people who start businesses who are not familiar with what a business plan actually is. As we mentioned before, these types of people go online and download a business plan template. Then, they fill in the blanks and voila, they have a written business plan!

Yes, it's true that you technically do have a business plan.

But how do you know whether you have a *good* plan for your business or not?

<u>Mapping the Journey</u>

If you want to drive from Calgary to Los Angeles, you need to map out how you are going to get there, right?

There are a number of route options you can take. You can choose to go a more direct inland route, or you can take the longer, more scenic route along the Oregon and Californian coast.

If you have kids, you might want to visit all the children's attractions along the way. Or if you are wine connoisseurs, you can stop off at the many wineries.

The bottom line is there are a number of different ways to get to your destination. Some are faster than others, but you end up at the same place no matter what.

When you are mapping out your vacation plans, many people will do research instead of just jumping into the car and driving (although some may jump in the car and go, which is what some new business owners try to do, too).

You may check the internet to see what is along the way and what the reviews are for specific locations and destinations. You may also ask friends or family who had previously taken the trip to get their recommendations. In the end, it's ultimately your decision as to which route you want to take.

Your business plan is your road map to your bigger vision. There are many ways to get there.

Most people want to find the fastest way to get to their financial success. But before you start looking at the "fastest way" to get there, you should research the different options available to you.

Instead of asking family and friends for their recommendations, you should ask business professionals. These are people who are familiar with the journey and can help you look at your options. They are the equivalent of the tourist visitor centers in all the hottest tourist cities.

Once you have a good idea of which route you want to take, it's an even better idea to write down the plan/route. This gives you a record of the plan. Without the plan written down, it is just an idea that you are interested in. Writing it down shows your commitment to the plan *and* gives you focus. It also gives you a visual of what pieces might not fit together or that are missing in the plan.

Your road map should also contain the justifications you used and the assumptions you made along the way to reach your decision.

It is a good idea to record the justifications in writing because, down the road, you may go back and ask yourself, "Why did I do this?"

If it's written down, then you know the method to your madness. Keep in mind that decisions are usually made based on the facts that are in front of you at the time. Over time, you will learn more, and your decisions may evolve based on new information. There are no right or wrong decisions; you make the best decisions based on the circumstances you are presented with at the time.

On your road trip, you may run into unexpected detours and construction zones.

For example, if there is a landslide on the road while you are driving through Glacier National Park, what should you do? You would need to assess the situation and make an educated decision for your next steps. This means you need to re-evaluate the given situation and make some course corrections.

This same thing happens with your business plan. You need to be flexible and course correct as often as is required. Sometimes it's just a detour, and other times it may mean adjusting the end destination based on new developments you have seen come up along the way.

In the end, it's all about being flexible and open-minded.

Creating the Road Map

The road map you create for your business is basically a giant glorified to-do list of the steps you need to take to get to your destination. To create this map, you need to start with the destination.

So, where is it that you want to go?

In business, your destination is your vision for where you want your company to go in the future. This is usually driven by your "why", the reason you want to start a business in the first place, and what your strong motivating factors are to make it happen.

Your "why" could be a significant event in your life that has shaped who you are today that makes you want to help people who are in similar situations.

After spending 23 years in the corporate world, I decided it was time to start a new chapter in my life. I didn't know what I wanted to do. One day, a colleague of mine, who got laid off from an oil and gas company, told me that he wanted to take his severance package and start a business. He knew what type of business he wanted to run but had no idea how to start. He asked whether I could help him.

Two month later, someone else asked me the same thing, whether I could help them start a business.

I started to see a pattern!

That's when I realized that the business concepts and knowledge I had acquired over the past twenty-three years were not common sense among the startup industry. Having an engineering degree, I naturally wanted to help solve people's problems and help them build their businesses. After all, this is what I was trained to do!

My vision for my company is to help business owners build a strong foundation from the start that allows them to find success faster. I want to improve the number of businesses that survive the first five years!

Knowing why you want to start your business can drive your overall vision. This is why I wake up in the morning, knowing that I am making an impact on someone's life.

This vision will be your ultimate destination. If your vision is still unclear, don't let it hold you back from starting your business. If you have a strong passion and drive to move forward, your "why" will eventually show up with a well-defined vision.

Don't be afraid or deterred if this vision changes a few times over the course of your starting phase in the business world, especially if you started your business with no real vision in mind.

Once you have your vision, create your mission to show how you plan to achieve this vision. Your vision and mission will outline your destination. You don't need to have this perfectly laid out in order to move ahead, and again, you shouldn't let that hold you back from starting if that is the case for you.

Now that you have your ultimate destination, it's time to create the road map.

Start by outlining the milestones you want to meet and by what deadline. These are the smaller destinations along the way.

On your way from Calgary to Los Angeles, you would start by getting to the Canadian border.

When starting your business, those smaller destinations on your road map might look like completing market research in order to get the validation you need in regard to whether you actually have a market for your product or not.

The "guts" of the road map are actually the specific step-by-step actions you will take to reach all of your milestones.

For example, to do the market research to find out if you have a market for your product/service, you might define your target market, define your product, and then do a survey of the target market.

The actual road map will entail details as to how this will happen — as we've mentioned above, who is going to do what, and by what date. Essentially, the road map is your outline/to-do list!

The most common milestones or stages for a road map are:

- **Market research** – Identify whether you have a product or service that people will want to buy.

- **Product structure and financial justification** – Evaluate how you will actually make money through this business venture.

- **Marketing and sales strategy** – How will you get clients?

- **Building infrastructure** - How will you create a foundation for your business to grow?

- **Profitability** – How will you make more money?

- **Growth** – How will you expand your services to meet your vision?

At each milestone on your journey, or even at different stages of your business, your road map will change based on the information you uncover in the previous milestones. The incredible thing about a road map is that it is constantly evolving. Some may find this frustrating, but this is the epitome of what growth in a business should be.

Download a business road map template for a startup business
www.NCPConsulting.net /5YearBizGuide

It is always a good idea to review/evaluate/analyze your road map every 3 to 6 months. As you are implementing the actions on your road map, you will uncover things that will affect the next phase of your business. If you are not constantly evaluating and analyzing what you already have, it will be much harder to envision and anticipate what the future might hold for your business.

One way to keep your business constantly growing and evolving is to take things one step at a time and course correct as often as needed. You want to make sure you are on track and not going off on a tangent that takes your business down a path you didn't need to venture down.

Turning Your Road Map into a Business Plan

A road map contains the step-by-step actions that need to be taken at the various stages of your business journey and why it makes sense. This is an internal document for you to follow.

A business plan is the formal document that contains the road map along with more sections relevant to how the business plan will be used. The most common reason why people need a business plan is to get financing from a lending source or secure investors that have expressed interest in your business.

This document will not only contain your road map; it will also have a financial forecast showing the potential for the business and justification on why this is a good investment for them. The financing chapter in this book will provide more details.

Basically, when it boils down to it, a business plan is a document to sell the merits of your business.

Unless you need to formally present your situation to someone for a specific reason, most business owners only need the road map as an internal document to help guide them.

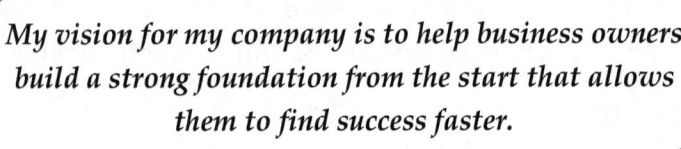

My vision for my company is to help business owners build a strong foundation from the start that allows them to find success faster.

Here are some quick tips for writing your road map or business plan:

- You are not writing a novel so bullet points are fine.

- If you get stuck on a question, move on. It will eventually come to you.

- Unless you are going for financing, there is no need to create a long-term plan. Focus on what you are going to do in the next three to six months first and foremost.

Once you have completed your road map or business plan, get an experienced business professional to review it.

These professionals should be able to validate your assumptions and make suggestions on how to improve your plan. Here's a word to the wise: leave your ego at the door no matter how much business experience you have.

Having another set of eyes to look at your plan means they will give you a different perspective based on their own experiences. It is not meant to be critical, but rather to open your mind to new ideas. It's quite possible that they have newer ideas that you've never thought of before, which can be a great thing for your overall business plan.

The person you have reviewing your plan should have experiences in different areas of business. Keep in mind that a sales and marketing expert may not be good at looking at the operational aspects of a business, or even the financial side. What this means is you might need more than one person to review your plan.

Take your time and do it right. Investing in a solid plan from the start will save you time and money, and create less stress for yourself in the long run.

Ideally, it would be good to find one person experienced in all areas, so they can take a holistic view of your business. You want to avoid playing whack-a-mole with your business where you fix one problem only to have another one pop up. Holistic viewpoints are the best way to go, if possible.

I have had people ask me, "If I pay you, will you review my business plan?"

I usually say "no".

If you send me a twenty-page business plan, what happens if, on page two, I think there is a different route option available that you never thought of? This means we will most likely have to throw out the remaining eighteen pages of your document.

You might feel discouraged, overwhelmed, or upset by this, in which case we've just wasted a massive amount of time.

Instead, I created a process that I know works.

The process I designed is unique in the way we create your business road map.

I have had many people who have come to me with one idea. By the time we were done, we had completely revamped how they were going to move forward. This is the power of collaboration in this process.

The areas covered are not unique. In fact, these areas are based on common business principles. The order in which the material is presented and how the process is facilitated is the strength of the program and what gets the business owner excited about their business. Together we make sure that all of the pieces feel right for you and not always what makes "logical" sense.

The last person to review your road map is your spouse or life partner. They may not be able to give you the professional opinion you need, and that is absolutely okay.

They need to understand what your plans are and how you plan to make money without spending all your hard-earned savings. This will give your partner the confidence to know that you know and understand what you are doing and how they can support you along the journey.

Remember that they are very much impacted by the decisions you make surrounding your business, so it's important to keep them in the loop at all times.

Now that you have a clear understanding of what a business road map and business plan can do for your business, you're ready to get started creating your own! The sky is truly the limit.

Download a business road map template for a startup business
www.NCPConsulting.net/5YearBizGuide

CHAPTER 4

CREATING A PRODUCT THAT SELLS

It's really no secret that the goal of starting a business is to create a product that sells.

If there is no need for the product, why would you start the business in the first place? It is never anyone's intention to create a business that will *lose* money. Everyone simply wants to do their due diligence up front and create something that people need and will buy, which will give us the biggest chance at success.

Let's start by figuring out exactly what people want. To do that, we need to know who we are selling to. This is what we call our **target market**. You will hear this term a great deal in the business world. This is the magic key to massive success.

Let's take a look at our solar system. In the center of our solar system we have the sun. Around the sun we have the planets. The planets rotate around the sun. If something happens to the sun, it will affect how the planets rotate around the sun. All of this sounds familiar, yes? You might be travelling back to your old science class days right now, and that's more than okay!

Our business is very much like the solar system. At the center of our business solar system is who we define as our **target market**.

There are three planets in our solar system. These planets are the product strategy, marketing message, and the sales and marketing strategy.

If we change our target market, the change will affect all three of these areas. For instance, a weight loss program for a high-performance athlete will look completely different to a weight loss program aimed at women after childbirth.

Yes, both people want to lose weight, but their reasons and needs are different.

The key to a successful business is to build a product that someone *wants* and *will* buy. If we don't know who we are selling to, then it's extremely difficult to build the product/service to fit who we want to serve.

It's time to explore the world of target markets in further detail.

Understanding Your Target Market

This is probably one of the hardest parts to get nailed down when starting any new business. There really is no right or wrong target market. All you're looking for is one group of people (also known as an audience) that is a better suited for you and your product /service.

If you change your target, how you structure your product may (and technically should) change.

Let's start by looking at why targeting your product to "everyone" doesn't always work.

I can understand that there are many groups that could potentially be attracted to your product, which means you don't want to lose out on business. But the reality is that you will end up being less successful because you will be spreading yourself too thin trying to serve everyone and no one at the same time.

Many years ago, I was diagnosed with high blood pressure. My doctor wanted me to lose weight. After three months of trying to lose the weight on my own, I wasn't getting any results. That's when I decided to hire a trainer.

Do you know how many fitness trainers are out there? It got to the point where my brain shut down because there were too many to choose from, and I did not know who to go with.

Then, one day, I met this trainer who told me they specialized in working with cardiac patients—those who have had heart attacks, strokes, and high blood pressure.

Bingo! That's who I went with.

He helped me control my blood pressure through nutrition and exercise for seven years, to the amazement of my hypertension specialist! Plus, I went from a size 14 to a size 2 at the same time. If it weren't for him specializing in people with my condition, I don't know if I would have gotten the same results.

Specializing in a certain area can be a good thing. You end up knowing your demographics really well, and you build a reputation as being the expert in that specific field.

This also means you might be able to charge more for your services. If you are in the computer service industry, there is no reason why you can't specialize in dental offices. You would not only know how to manage their computer systems; you would also be able to support the common software dentists use. What this means is that your clients don't pay for your learning time, as it's your area of expertise.

They're getting more bang for their buck if they look at it the right way.

Remember I said that your marketing strategy is dependent on your target market? Different target markets will hang out at different places. Can you afford the time to be going from place to place incorporating different strategies?

It's easier to focus your efforts on **one** strategy. Give it some time to work. Then, if you decide it's not working, re-evaluate and course correct accordingly.

If you spread yourself too thin with too many strategies, you won't give any of the strategies a chance to mature and actually work for you.

Many people I work with may have two target markets **maximum**.

Having two target markets *is* manageable, but it will still take work to incorporate possibly two very different strategies for your marketing.

For example, a health practitioner may have their main focus on getting more patients. However, they may also focus on building partnerships with other health practitioners that have complementary practices. This would be their secondary target market.

You may see chiropractors partnering with massage therapists as they both have complementary services to help patients with their pain management. How you attract massage therapists will be different to how you attract chiropractic patients. However, both business partners will achieve the same result of getting more clients into the practice.

Another common example is deciding whether your target market is children or parents when you have a child-oriented product or service. Keep in mind that you need to capture the interest of the child, AND you will need to justify to the parent why this is a good investment.

Ultimately, the parent is the final decision maker as they are the ones that pay the bill. This means the parent is the *true* target market in the end.

It's also important to remember that just because you specialize in a specific group doesn't mean you don't accept business from the other groups. All it really means is that your advertising is geared towards the original group.

For example, I once met a realtor who specializes in helping divorced couples sell off the family home and purchase new, separate homes. She went through a divorce herself and understands the sensitivity of the situation.

If someone is referred to her to sell their home and they are not going through a divorce, she would absolutely say yes to the business! Just because this person is not her target market doesn't mean she won't service them. It just means she is not actively promoting herself to that particular market.

Selecting a Target Market

This is not always an easy task to do. If you find yourself struggling to identify who your target market truly is, here are some simple questions to help guide you through the process:

- What industry do you know really well? Have you spent many years working in a certain industry where you have a wealth of knowledge and experience in?

- Go through your top revenue-generating clients since you started your business. Do they have anything in common? Where did you meet them? Are they all in the service industry? Are they all men? All women?

- If you offer more than one product or service, which one is the most profitable? This is not necessarily the one that is bringing in the most money. Once you have removed your expenses, which one makes you the most money? Once you know that, then determine which demographics would most likely buy this product based on this information.

- What are your hobbies, and where do you spend most of your time? For example, if you enjoy ballroom dancing and you compete in this sport, is there an opportunity for your product or service among this group? Or are you a hockey mom that spends her days at the skating rink?

- Where is your comfort zone? If you prefer to work with women instead of men, then go with women.

- What do you have personal experience in? If you have raised kids, then you might want to consider targeting families. A single person who has never had a child will have less credibility with families than a mother or father.

- What are your lifestyle interests? Are you a foodie who hangs out at the latest up and coming restaurants? Or are you a photographer that spends time at photo groups?

Did you notice that many of questions above look at your own personal life? This may seem like an odd way to approach finding your target market, but it's important to try and find a demographic that is a natural fit for you.

If you enjoy something, find a way to make it work for you. What you don't want to do is to try and stick a square peg into a round hole. You are going to be spending a great deal of time with these people during the course of your business, so it's good for you to be comfortable in the environment from the beginning.

> *It's really no secret that the goal of starting a business is to create a product that sells.*

<u>Defining Your Target Market</u>

This is where you write down the details of your target market. The more details you give, the stronger your product will become. Below is a list to help you get started:

- Gender
- Age range
- Income level
- Marital status
- Family situation
- Occupation
- Education level
- Lifestyle
- Behaviors
- Buying patterns
- Hobbies
- Values

If your target market is another business, then the above profile should be on the owner or decision maker of the business. You will also need to profile the business itself. Below are the typical characteristics for profiling the business:

- Number of employees
- Revenue range
- Company type
- Number of years in business
- Stage of their business
- Their struggles
- Industry

Many people find that this exercise works best in a group environment. I created collaborative workshops that give people an opportunity to explore different target markets in a group environment. Each one of us has had different experiences, and this collaborative process allows us to dig deeper into the definition of their target market. The better you know your target market, the stronger your product will become.

Once you have defined your target market, you should research to find out how large the market is. If you have an ultra-luxury item, your target market might be small in your community, but larger if you have an international scope.

Understanding the Goals of the Target Market

Now that we have defined your target market in detail, it should be easy to come up with a list of what is important for these people. What is causing them grief in their life, and what are their dreams and goals?

Your number one goal is to solve their pain points!

If a person is trying to lose weight, what is their true reason? Is it because they want to gain confidence, so they can get the promotion at work? Or is it that they want to be pain free, so they can play with their young kids in the yard?

The motivation level is different between these two groups of people, which is why defining your target market is so vital.

For the chiropractor, their clients may want to be pain free. The massage therapists that the chiropractor wants to partner with will want to find ways to grow their business and make more money. Again, these are two very different goals. The chiropractor will need to address both.

By clearly articulating the goals of your target market and their pain points or barriers to achieving their goals, you will have defined the sun in your solar system. This is the basis of the product or service you create, your marketing message, and the strategy you use to sell your solution.

Your number one goal is to solve their pain points!

Researching Your Solution

Now that you know who you are targeting and what their goals are, you should do some preliminary research. This research will give you a stronger product to meet your target market's needs and help you determine how to position yourself in the industry so that you can stand out in the crowd!

- **Direct competitors** – Who offers similar solutions to yours? What are their strengths and weaknesses? How are they pricing their product or service? You can get a lot of this information off the internet by putting in different keyword searches in a search engine. Think of yourself as the client and what keywords would they use. Record your findings.

- **Indirect competitors** – These are the companies that offer services that can achieve the same results as your business can, but are in a different industry. For example, you might be a fitness trainer that helps people lose weight. You may be indirectly competing with nutritionists or weight loss products that are trying to achieve the same results with your target market.

- **Your strengths** – These are the strengths of your company and of you personally. What do you bring to the table? Is it that you have over 10 years of experience in the industry, your bubbly personality, or your strong organizational skills?

- **Your weaknesses** – No one is perfect. This exercise is really about identifying the areas you need to work on, so your business can become stronger. If you dislike accounting, then you can create an action item to find a good bookkeeper to help you. If you don't have testimonials, then how are you going to get some?

- **Opportunity** – What are some of the opportunities that can impact your business? If house prices start coming down, it could mean more opportunities to sell investment properties to investors? Or if you have a very hot summer, your lemonade stand will do very well!

- **Threats** – What are the negative factors that can impact your business? If the economy is bad, and there are a lot of layoffs in the industry, this could impact your sales to that market. It can also impact the amount consumers are spending on luxury items.

By understanding the above factors, you will be able to create a stronger product for your target market.

Creating Your Product

Now that you have a good idea of who you are creating a solution for and what their goals are, it's time to put together your solution for them.

Let's start by looking at what other solutions are currently available for them. These are the other competing solutions out there.

The key to your success is to define how you are different from the other solutions, and why they should come to you instead of going to the others.

If you cannot find a niche that makes you different, then you are just like everyone else. When you find your secret sauce, that's when your business will start to explode. You will elevate yourself onto a different platform and change the game.

Sometimes this means specializing in a certain area, or going after a market that has few competitors. If there are few competitors, then it could mean either people have not been successful in this market and they abandoned it, or that it's a new, untapped market. You should review your research and talk to your target market to see which one it is.

Your unique differentiator could be a process you created that gives results, or it could be a different way of approaching a common problem.

Regardless of what your secret sauce is, the key is to find it. Many people have difficulties with this part. Sometimes all it takes is finding a business professional that can help you design a product that is uniquely you.

When I began working with startup businesses, I realized that there were many companies offering training programs to help educate the new business owner. I found that people were getting overwhelmed with the amount of information and did not know how to apply it directly to their business.

They were given templates to fill in the blanks, and they were still unsure whether they were going in the right direction or not. The Kickstart Program I developed gave people the quick answers they were looking for. This resulted in them selling their products with more confidence and getting better results. The Kickstart Program became my secret sauce.

Once you have figured out what your unique differentiator is, you should validate everything you have put together. You would most likely have only been making assumptions along the way.

For example, we assumed the goals of your target market. It's time to actually validate all your assumptions before you sink more time and money into your business venture. If you don't get the results you had hoped for, then you need to reconsider your strategy. If you get positive results, then you have landed on a gold mine, and it's time to take it to the next level!

CHAPTER 5

GETTING CLIENTS

Very few people have unlimited time and money to spend on sales and marketing, especially if they are still in the startup stage of their business. If this sounds like you, you should carefully design a plan that will make the best use of your time and give you the biggest bang for your buck.

What Exactly is Sales and Marketing?

I could never understand why "sales and marketing" is naturally referred to in this order. Technically, you need to do marketing before sales. Let's explore the difference between the two terms.

If you are a fisherman on a boat, the ultimate goal is to catch a fish and bring it onto the boat, correct? This is the same goal for a business. We want someone to buy our product or service.

To start, the fisherman will put the bait on the hook and throw it into the water. The purpose of the bait is to attract the fish to the hook. This is the equivalent of marketing, where we are attracting people to our store, website, or to pick up the phone to call us.

In marketing, there are a number of different ways to attract "prospects" to our solution. A prospect is someone who is interested in what we have to offer and hasn't bought anything from you yet.

Once the fish takes the bait and bites on the hook, the fisherman starts to reel it in. They cannot go too fast or the fish will jump off the hook, nor can they go too slow or the fish will wiggle its way off. The object is to have just the right technique, so you can get the fish into the boat.

The process to get the fish into the boat, once the fish has taken the bait, is the equivalent to the sales process.

This is exactly like your first interaction with the prospect. It can be when you answer the phone, start an email conversation from their web inquiry, or when you first meet them at a networking event, shake hands and say "it's nice to meet you".

Once you have made that first contact, you have entered the sales process with the ultimate goal of getting that person to buy your product or service.

When it comes to getting people to buy your product or service, you need to have a marketing strategy to attract them to your solution. Then, you need to employ your sales skills to get them to sign on the dotted line.

Having these two components is very important to your sales and marketing strategy, but if you want to accelerate your results, you need to also have the third component, which is a strong marketing message. Without a message filled with your marketing strengths, you may still get results, but they may not come to fruition quite as quickly as you had hoped.

The process to get the fish into the boat, once the fish has taken the bait, is the equivalent to the sales process.

Your Marketing Message

The purpose of a marketing message is to attract people to your product or service and to stand out among the crowd.

Many people think this message is simply telling people about their product or service. You can do that, but it's not always effective. Telling people that you are a realtor will get a response of "that's nice". The problem is, you are probably one out of thousands of realtors in your city. So, what makes you stand out from the rest?

If you focus on "what you can do for them" and show them how you are different up front, then you will have caught their attention and shortened the time it will take to sell to this person. If this person does not engage in your message, that's perfectly okay, because they may not be your target market, *or* they are not currently interested in what you are selling.

One thing that you must get used to in the business world is the fact that not everyone is going to buy from you—not from the get go or in the far future. Your product or service may not be what they want or need, and you have to be okay with that from the start!

To put together an engaging marketing message that will catch a person's attention, here is the formula:

- **Target market** - Who is your solution for?

- **Their goals or challenges** – What are their pain points and/or what are their dreams?

- **Your unique differentiator and solution** – How are you different from everyone else out there with similar solutions?

Let's look at the realtor example more closely.

A realtor can have diverse target markets with different messaging strategies. When they are talking to sellers, they might lead with making the process of selling the home stress-free as well as getting a good price for their home. Or, for the home buyer target market, the realtor should be focused on selling the client with helping them to find a place to call home and build family memories in. The realtor may even focus on real estate investors, which means they will talk more about increasing the investor's asset portfolio and building cash flow.

So out of the three messages above, which one would you want to advertise? If you use all three, it could potentially confuse people.

To avoid any confusion on the potential client's side, choose one message to advertise and be known as the expert in that field. Find a differentiator to make yourself stand out, and people will remember you for it. You don't have to give up working with the other two target markets, but they won't be your main marketing focus.

Think of a recruiter who is looking at resumes. After the first 30, they start to all blend in and look alike. You need to make yours stand out!

Here are some extra tips to help you stand out:

- **Tell a memorable story** - People remember stories, and they will enforce your message.

- **End with a call to action** – "If this sounds like you, then call me or come see me!"

- **Create a catchy phrase** – I am fully aware that this is easier said than done. However, this will eventually come to you, so don't let it hold you back if you don't have one yet.

- **Focus on the benefits** - What will your solution do for your target market?

- **Be consistent** – If people hear the same message from you over and over again, you will be known as the expert and go-to person on that subject.

- **Write everything down** – This includes customer reactions, so you know what worked and what didn't for the future.

- **Continually improve your message** – Be open to new ideas that will help make your message stronger. Nothing is ever perfect.

- **Have multiple version of the same message** – People may get bored hearing the same message repeatedly, so mix it up!

Once you have created your message, it is a good idea to test it out on your friends and your target market first. If you get a reaction that resembles a "tell me more" attitude, then you know you are on the right track.

When I started telling people that I help the overwhelmed business owner get clarity and direction, I found that people who resonated with this message would say, "That's me!"

It quickly showed me who may be the right candidate for my service and shortened my sales cycle.

If you are not getting this type of reaction, then keep adjusting your message until you get it just right. Sometimes having an outside perspective will get you better results.

The process I created to get a powerful marketing message is probably the strongest part of my program. Once you get this message right, your confidence will increase and you will get better results.

> *Tell a memorable story - People remember stories, and they will enforce your message.*

Where to Use Your Marketing Message

You use your marketing message everywhere!! This is called branding—putting out the same consistent look and message in everything you do.

Here is a list of places you can incorporate your message easily and effectively:

- **Introductions** – When you are introduced to someone, and they ask you what you do.

- **The elevator pitch** – An introduction to a group of people, typically at a networking event. Thirty seconds is not a lot of time if you have a lot to say. If you don't know what to say and wind up improvising, thirty seconds can seem like an eternity!

- **One-minute pitch** – An extension of your thirty-second pitch by adding a memorable story or anecdote,

- **Speaking engagements** – This is the introduction used when people announce you as the next speaker on the state.

- **Website content** – This is what to put on your website.

- **Email signature** – Remind people at the end of all your email messages.

- **Business card** – Putting a memorable tagline will remind people what you can do for them when they see your card.

- **Letterhead** – Include it everywhere, even on invoices and proposals. Make sure it reinforces your look and message.

- **LinkedIn profile** – People like to check out a person's background on LinkedIn. It is like your resume.

- **Social media** – This could be from banners on your business page or a stamp on all of your posts.

People need to see your message at least seven times before they will remember it, so plaster it everywhere!

To keep your look consistent, seriously consider your selection of colors, logos, and design. If you are stuck and can't find a logo you like, don't let it hold you back from starting your business. Nobody ever bought a product just because it had a cool logo. It's what you promise to deliver that's more important.

If you want to spend the money for a logo, there are many designers out there that can create you one. Note that designers tend to have a style. Look and see what the designer has created in the past and compare it to the type of designs you like.

Now that you have a marketing message and design, it's time to get the word out and find yourself some clients!

Where to Find Clients

The strategy you use to find clients is really dependent on where your clients hang out.

Conversely, where your clients hang out is dependent on who your target market is.

A twenty-five-year-old single, business professional climbing the corporate ladder will be hanging out at much different places than the forty-year-old stay-at-home mother of young kids.

It could very well be the after-work bar scene vs the local community parks and school functions. Even a thirty-five-year-old female with a young family will have a different lifestyle compared to a fifty-three-year-old empty nester.

When we are looking at marketing activities, we need to understand where these people are physically going and what their online digital habits are. Then you choose the best method that will get you in front of them.

There are many unique ways to market to your target market. There are traditional marketing methods and there are "outside the box", creative methods to get a person's attention.

Here is a good mix of some ideas to get you started:

Direct Marketing Strategies:

- **Cold calling** - Making direct contact with prospects based on research.

- **Networking events** - Attending events to meet prospects. Choose events that have your target market and where you feel comfortable with the people in the room.

- **Directory listings** - Be part of a directory aimed at your target market. Ideally, the directory listing should allow space for a description, so you can say how you are unique.

- **Direct email campaigns** - This requires you to create a collection of contact names and email addresses for people to opt into. This is a cost effective way to communicate with a group of people but keep in mind that this is becoming ineffective as people are getting bombarded with too many emails.

- **Direct mail campaigns** - Traditional mail campaigns can be costly, so make sure it is a targeted campaign, and that you have a strong message to give. Target addresses based on different demographics are typically available for purchase.

- **Trade shows** - Either attend the event as a participant or a vendor to get contacts.

- **Social media advertising** – This can be paid or organic traffic.

- **Google Adwords** – This is paid advertising based on keyword searches into Google.

- **Promotional items** – Pens, calendars, etc. - this can be costly and have little return. It is most effective as a reminder to people who already know you.

- **Media advertising** – Magazine, radio, TV, newspaper, transit, and community newsletters. This can be costly, but can also get you a large coverage.

- **Public advertising** – This would include things such as vehicle stickers, road signs, billboards, and road banners. Keep in mind that you only have three to four seconds to get your message and contact information across to drivers.

Indirect Strategies:

- **Referral programs** - Potentially can reduce your marketing and advertising costs.

- **Partnerships** - Creative ways to get referrals.

- **Social media blogging** - This shows you are an expert in your area.

- **Press releases (PR)** - Announcements that can catch media attention in all the right ways.

- **Sponsorship** - Get your name out at events that have your target audience as attendees.

- **Seminars/Workshops** – Speaking to your target audience or attend an event with your target market.

- **Association memberships** - This would be for associations for your target market, not for your industry.

- **Publishing** - Papers, books, and media articles will show that you are an expert in your area.

- **Conduct Surveys** - Get in front of your target market and show them you are interested in what they have to say.

When putting together marketing campaigns, it's a good idea to keep track of your results.

If one method is not giving you results, then try something else. Keep in mind that you need to give it time to work before changing. Sometimes it could take up to one year to build the relationships at a networking event before getting a return on your investment. Track your progress, be patient, and change what is not working.

Track your progress, be patient, and change what is not working.

Brand Your Company and Set the Bar Higher in Your Business

It is said, in the world of entrepreneurial life, that the person who follows their heart has the key to success.

Lorraine Shulba has known that – an over 20-year expert in her field - illustrator, graphic designer and entrepreneur has run her business, Little Bug Studios, with that same notion successfully for 17 years!

She wants you to ask:

- **What is your graphic design saying about you in the world?**
- **What sets you apart as an entrepreneur in your field of expertise?**
- **What is your branding saying about you and your business?**

Graphic design is one of those marketing and business needs that can speak volumes about you and what you stand for in your business.

You know the statement; a picture is worth a 1,000 words; well, what happens if your graphic design does not represent you well – executed unsuccessfully? It can lead to thousands of dollars in lost business!

Lorraine's work is award winning, and she "sees" who you are from the words you choose on how to describe your heart, your business and vision. Once this is captured, your message is very unique to the world and can set you apart by leaps and bounds.

Lorraine states, by defining your brand and reflecting your power in your marketing materials as the professional you are, you set yourself up for success. You are demonstrating that you are the right person for your potential clients and showcasing yourself as the expert in your field. Design and optics are the center of your marketing and branding. The promise to deliver with your services can be absolutely established with amazing, award winning design – this combo can make your business go BOOM with productivity!

Myths about graphic design:

1. Anyone with canva can create a good design
2. People don't judge you by your graphic design
3. Curb appeal does not get you business - BIG FALACY!

The benefits of great graphic design:

1. **Reputation** - if your graphic design is not of professional quality, it can represent a negative impression of your business. It can state that you don't care, and people want to feel important and valued.

2. **Message** - your messaging is key when you are building a business, and solid graphic design can emulate your message to the world. People are drawn to visuals and how it makes them feel.

3. **Enhance** how you communicate with people - your image can speak volumes to your clients.

4. **Serves** to convey your ideas in a way that's effective and beautiful

5. **Makes you look good** - when you invest in solid branding and design, it represents you and your company as being solid and reputable.

6. **Message of credibility and professionalism** - it means you care about how you are viewed and seen in the public eye. It emulates success and confidence!

7. **Consistent imagery resonates** - when your picture is on a banner with your company name, you want to be proud of what you have created; your branding needs to flow form

8. **Memorable brand identity** - when branding flows from your website to your banners on display to your PowerPoint presentation. This means business and success will result in increased sales and referrals for you.

9. **Representing your brand** - when you have alignment to your business and your graphics in your branding, online and offline, people will seek you out to work with you.

Too often, Lorraine Shulba, has seen business owners try to do it themselves - graphic design and branding. They spend money on software and hours trying to figure it out with only mediocre design and expression. They don't get the results the want from their website or advertisements because people are not resonating with what they represent.

Your branding is your identity in the online and offline world. People go to websites to research you. If they don't like what they see, they won't choose to work with you, regardless of how knowledgeable you may be.

Lorraine has extensive experience, not only in design, but also illustration. How would a professionally illustrated logo, picture or custom picture speak for your brand and set you apart from your competition?

The power of graphic design and knowing its importance emulates in all of your messaging, which represents you at a higher level than someone that did not invest, or tried to do it themselves.

There is a time and a place for doing your own graphics; however, when it is the first impression people see on your website, magazine, bill board, book cover, brochure, your want it to be epic and by taking your graphic design, logo and marketing seriously. People will understand your sincerity and your message way more clearly, and will set you apart in the market place, which will result in more clients for you and your business.

**Download the 5 things to consider
when branding your business at
www.bluebugstudios.com/5YearBizGuide**

Publishing a Book

As an entrepreneur, there are many aspects to your business that require your attention. Being able to talk about your story and why you do what you do is often understated. The world is busy, both online and offline, and you must set yourself apart as an expert in your field. Heather Andrews is the founder of the Follow It Thru Publishing, and she helps people bring their story to life to leverage their message and create more visibility through books, audiobooks, and podcasts.

According to www.entrepreneur.com, publishing a book can help you gain the attention you need. They also state that publishing a book is the most underutilized method used to gain visibility, attention, and credibility.

By publishing a book, a business owner gains media coverage (podcast interviews, speaking events), and it helps create authority for your product or service. It is a multipurpose tool which can offer an additional revenue stream. There are different viewpoints on whether a book can be used as a business card. Some believe it shouldn't be used. Heather disagrees. Everyone has a business card, but not everyone has a book. A book is an investment, a marketing tool and should be treated as an asset in your business that you can sell for revenue.

Heather shares how your published book can gain attention for your business:

1. **Expertise** - People refer to books to find knowledge and guidance.

2. **Media coverage** - In the last year, the average person has increased the number of podcasts they listen to from five to seven per week.

3. **Visibility** - Entrepreneur.com states that "Amazon is the number one search engine. 44% of product and services searches begin there."

You want your book to reflect your best work, input, value, and knowledge. When people find value in your work, they will refer their colleagues to you. Heather Andrews, who is a bestselling author on Amazon, knows that when she is introduced as a bestselling author, her expert status increases.

Heather Andrews teaches her clients how to make revenue from their book by creating communities, collaborating and impacting others.

- A physical book to sell at event and trade shows.
- Audiobook sales- Good ereader.com states a 31% increase in audiobook sales in the last three years.
- A Video/e-course based on book content to sell.
- Workshops based on book content.
- Speaking events to share your knowledge.
- Publishing a book is a marketing tool and can save you on taxes.

In the world of entrepreneurship, it's common to do things alone, but publishing a book is a lengthy process that could mean time away from your business. Heather Andrews believes that publishing a book requires careful planning to ensure its success. Remember, the book will be a reflection of you and your business.

Steps to publishing a book:

- Topic outlining
- Content building
- Editing, copy-editing, and proofreading
- Cover and layout design
- Formatting
- Distribution
- Marketing

Each step of the process is a person you need to hire if you want your book to be a well-received reflection of your business. Follow It Thru Publishing can take care of every step efficiently and professionally.

Heather's system will save you time and, in turn, money.

What are the different ways to publish?

1. Self-publishing

- Cost-effective.
- No need to query an agent or publisher.
- Time-consuming unless you hire people for each step.
- Hard to gain visibility without marketing help.
- Can be overwhelming.

2. <u>Traditional publishing</u>

Pros

- Validation.
- Easier for print copy distribution in stores.
- Established team.
- No upfront cost.

Cons

- Querying takes time and can be disheartening.
- Process can be slower.
- You may not keep the rights to your book.
- You will only earn a small percentage of each sale.
- You may still have to do your own marketing.

Follow It Thru Publishing is a hybrid system with a specialized team. Their goal is to help you publish so you can use your book to share your story and knowledge and leverage it as a business. Heather and her team take away the cost and stress, so you can be free to concentrate on your business.

Download the top ten things to consider when publishing at
www.followitthrupublishing.com/5YearBizGuide

You want your book to reflect your best work, input, value, and knowledge

Digital Marketing and How It Will Benefit Your Business

Before we jump into **digital marketing,** Catherine Saykaly-Stevens of The Networking Web wants us to understand that marketing is nothing more than a form of communication.

Most are familiar with **traditional marketing** where you have seen plenty of ads bought for print; mainly flyers, magazines, and newspapers (radio and television ads too).

Before the internet became available to the masses, traditional marketing had three limitations:

- Simple exchange of money for one-time exposure (or a set number of times).

- Single direction of communication from the ad source to the masses.

- Small focus on demographics (stats), geographic (location), or psychographics (behaviors).

While traditional marketing is still alive today, it has shrunk considerably with great competition from digital marketing.

What is Digital Marketing?

Digital marketing is simply the promotion of your products, services, programs, books, events, etc., through any one or many forms of electronic media (or also known as channels).

Catherine Saykaly-Stevens explains that digital marketing should include a plan to execute, a campaign to run, and the results monitored and analyzed. This way the campaign may be altered and improved to ensure better future results.

Many people believe that digital marketing channels are solely social media channels like Facebook, Instagram, LinkedIn,

YouTube, Twitter, etc. While social media is certainly included, there are many other channels to consider, such as:

- Social media marketing
- Content marketing
- Search engine optimization (SEO)
- Search engine marketing (SEM)
- Pay-per-click (PPC)
- Pay-per-view (PPV)
- Facebook ads
- Paid advertising
- Affiliate marketing
- Joint venture partnerships (JVP)
- Email marketing automation
- Landing pages and funnels
- Online PR and interviews

More channels exist, and new opportunities are always coming soon.

Yes, this is a lot to take in!

To complicate matters further, we blast the three limitations of traditional marketing. Since the internet's availability to the masses, and with escalating capacity, digital marketing includes:

- Numerous opportunities for exposure for pay, for exchange, and for free.

- Multiple directions of communication, including giving voice to the audience, the consumer, and to negative comments through multiple channels with the ability to directly influence the original source.

- Laser focus on demographics, geographic, and psychographics, and the ability to target ideal audiences in their preferred channels.

Let's simplify what we have so far.

How Does Digital Marketing Work for my Business?

Digital marketing is simply **your** campaign strategy that you plan and execute to effectively communicate your specific business message to your ideal audience in their preferred channel(s).

How Many Digital Channels Should I Use?

Catherine says to work with as many as you can afford the time, money, and effort to run.

Here are five good digital channel rules that she shares:

- **Be where your audience is** - There is no point in building numerous (text) blogs if your entire audience solely embraces video.

- **Set your LinkedIn account** - LinkedIn is your professional online social media platform and where influencers will seek you out. You can set it and forget it, or invest time daily.

- **Assistance** - If you're not an expert in what you plan to do and are pressed for time, seek assistance and do it right the first time.

- **Get success with one digital channel first** -You can always create your channels (complete the bios and headers), and then post honestly about where you spend the bulk of your time. When your primary channel is working and bringing your ideal audience to you, work on the next.

- **Do your due diligence** – Get to know your keywords; not just your industry keywords, but what your audience uses to find you. This is how you show up in searches.

How Will I Know If My Campaign Worked?

Catherine explains that your campaign must elicit a response from your audience. These responses are your results. If you do not like your results, monitoring and improvements from the start lead to better future results.

What Would You Consider a Win?

She gives some examples of results you may want:

- Gain signatures
- Get more blog subscriptions
- Enlarge number of volunteers
- Expand online visibility and reach
- Attract influencers
- Obtain interviews, podcasts, and media
- Increase followers
- Grow your mailing list
- Convert to sales and gain more clients

Whether only one or all of the above is what you consider success, each requires individual implementation, monitoring, and alterations in your campaign.

As with digital channels, focusing on the success of one thing at a time is better than implementing all at once.

The 80/20 Rule and Digital Marketing

The 80/20 rule applies to digital marketing in the same way as other areas.

Catherine explains that whatever the amount of time it took for you to create your product, service, program, book, events, etc.(i.e. if you were to spend <u>80% more time on marketing</u> your item), you will improve your success rate and the results you desire.

In conclusion, digital marketing is complex and may waste your valuable time, money, and effort. However, digital marketing may also bring you results beyond what you ever imagined possible.

Catherine explains that the key is in your strategy; the planning, execution, monitoring, and the alterations of your digital marketing campaign.

Download digital marketing campaign strategies and a simple digital marketing campaign example for you to implement at www.TheNetworkingWeb.com/5YearBizGuide

Your campaign must elicit a response from your audience. These responses are your results.

Sales Skills

Now that you have caught the attention of your prospective clients, it's time for the sales process to start.

There are many different sales styles and it's a matter of finding the one that works best for you and your personality.

Some people use the "buy now" technique, which is typically used by speakers on a room full of strangers.

Others use a softer sell. This is where you build the relationship with your prospect and become a consultant to them. It's really about you helping them find a solution to their problems – which, coincidentally, is your product or service!

You should take the time to understand what is important to your clients, and the underlying reason why they want a solution to their problem in the first place. The better you know your prospect, the higher the chance is of you receiving the sale.

People like to buy things from people they know, like, and trust. In fact, in sales and marketing, this is one of the biggest concepts that business owners must master. There are many people that may offer a similar solution as you do, and that is okay. This is why relationship building is key. If the client is looking for a realtor, and you are the only realtor that they have built a relationship with, they will most likely to call you first.

To make the sales process go faster, consider mastering some of these techniques:

- **Identify the decision makers** – If the wife typically consults with the husband on a large purchase like a house, then make sure both are present during all decision making times. You don't want to delay the process of constantly having to go back and forth between the two.

- **Always focus on the benefits to your prospect** – Rather than telling them about how great your product is, focus on what it will do for them. Keep reminding them repeatedly. And then remind them some more.

- **A person needs to connect with you seven times to remember you** – You can't just present your solution once and expect the person to buy (unless you are selling a commodity product that is based on an impulse buy – like red shoes!). Find at least seven ways to contact your prospect and stay in front of them as much as possible. This is how you will make an impression on them.

- **You must ask for the sale** – This is arguably one of the most difficult parts to a sales strategy any business owner will have to face. You can't just present what you have and then walk away, hoping they will buy. You have to actually ask them- "Would you like to buy one?", "Do you prefer the red or the blue one?", or "When would you like to get started?" If they are not ready to take the next step, they will let you know. Remember to ask often without being pushy. You will get more sales this way.

- **Be prepared for objections** – When going into a sales conversation without understanding that objections will arise is like walking into a test without studying. Neither of these situations will end well. To be better prepared, write a list of all the reasons why you think people will tell you why they don't want to buy your product. Prepare some responses to the counters. Then incorporate the counters into your message and address it before it even comes up in conversation.

- **Be prompt with your follow up and always keep your word** – This will build your credibility and prove that you are reliable. It also displays to your potential client that you have integrity and punctuality which keeps you front and center with your prospect so they don't forget you.

- **Dot your i's and cross your t's** – The presentation of your emails and proposals reflect your attention to detail. Make sure spelling and grammar are checked, and your document is professional looking and properly formatted before hitting send (this is good practice no matter what you're sending off).

- **Address the person by the right name** – Some people are particular when it comes to their name. You don't want to offend someone when they prefer to be called Richard instead of Rick. In today's world, there are also unusual spellings of common names. Ensure you are addressing the person properly.

- **Track your conversations** – As your business expands, your prospect and client list will also grow. It will become much harder to remember who likes what and how many kids they have. Your tracking systems can be sheets of paper in a binder or a note system. You may even opt for a full blown CRM (customer relationship manager) system/program. It doesn't matter what system you use, as long as it works for you.

If you are not familiar with the sales process, find someone to help you put the pieces together and role play. This could be a business professional, colleague or friend. Practicing in front of a mirror also help. This will help you build confidence and accelerate your results.

Targeting Businesses

If your target market is another business, it's probably going to be a little more complicated for you.

First of all, your target market profile should tell you what type of business you are targeting. If you are targeting small businesses where you are dealing directly with the owner and they only have one or two employees, you are probably going to follow the rules outlined above.

If your target market is large corporations, there will be a level of strategic account planning involved. The sales process now becomes a game of chess where you are not only selling a product or service, you must also understand the dynamics and politics within the organization, who has the decision making power, who can influence the decision even though they are not the final approving authority, and what your competitors are doing in the account.

This was my world for the first 7 years of my career selling corporate business systems to oil and gas companies. We had a sales team involved and we strategically paired our people up with the appropriate person in the account.

In these situations, it's a good idea to get another set of professional eyes on the situation. You only have one opportunity to get your million dollar deal. Increase your chances with the proper planning.

If you are offering a brand new solution that has not been tested and proven, and you have not had your first client yet, then you might want to consider starting with a small to mid-sized company first to get things off the ground. They are usually more flexible if things don't go as planned.

With the large corporations, you probably only have one opportunity to get it right so you want to make sure you have everything in order before you knock on their door.

Large companies usually have a formal vendor vetting process. Make sure you familiarize yourself with their corporate policies. Also, be aware that sometimes large companies have more red tape than a smaller one. Their approval process is longer, and there are typically more people involved in the decision. This is the price you have to pay to play with the big boys. The return, however, will probably be worth the extra time and effort.

If you are not comfortable with the corporate sales process, then consider getting help from someone who specializes in this type of sales training. In the end, it's just a matter of going out and actually talking to people to get your own personal experience.

Taking Care of Your Clients

Did you know that the time and money you will spend to get a new client is very high? This is the price you pay to grow your company.

Did you also know that if you take good care of your existing clients and they rave about your product or service, they can become your best salesperson? They won't hesitate to refer people to you because of the great experience you gave them. These are things people won't forget and would happily share.

When they are in this state of mind, this is a good time to ask for a testimonial. Getting it in writing to share on your website is one thing, but it will go further if they go out of their way to post a Google review or Linkedin recommendation for you. These are things you cannot fake.

Simple things like continuously following up to see how they are doing and how you might be able to help them, will go a long way. Show you understand their needs and sincerely care about their growth.

It is the little things that you do for people that will keep you at the top of their mind. It helps build your reputation in the industry, and eventually people will hear through word of mouth, which will make life easier for you.

CHAPTER 6

EXPERT CHAPTER CONTRIBUTOR

Darlene Hull of
HotSpot Social Media

Darlene Hull is an aficionado of social media for the overworked, overwhelmed and underfunded. Once you've got that covered, your next step is her other passion: the automation of your business. Hey, It's all about the freedom!

CHAPTER 6

THE CRAZY ART OF SOCIAL MEDIA

There you are, standing in all your frazzled glory as an entrepreneur, spinning your business plates on so many poles to keep up with your business plan, organizing client deliverables, balancing your books, increasing your knowledge and facility in your chosen field. Then some crazy person comes up and says, "You need to also be on social media."

The plates smash, the poles fall down, your hat falls off, and there you are in a crumpled heap wondering how you can add one more thing (and social media is a sizable thing at that!) to your daily plan.

Let's not even mention the fact that social media changes faster than the weather forecast, and suddenly you've got a problem on your hands.

But really, do you *need* social media?

Well, no, not if you've already got an unending supply of leads, all the market research necessary to provide the best product for your perfect target market, and a whole mass of raving fans that can't shut up about you.

But if you're like most businesses, you don't have all that, and so, yes, you need social media. Here's what it gives you:

- A huge resource for finding and connecting with the kinds of people you'd LIKE to do business with.

- A chance to show off as an industry thought leader, or at least a very competent worker in your field.

- An easy way for your raving fans to share how wonderful you are to a whole stream of people you might not ever have a connection to otherwise.

- A legitimate way to spy on your ideal target market to better understand their needs and the language they use to talk about their ideal solutions to that problem (the marketing mother lode, for sure).

- A way to build relationships with your target audience without ever getting out of your pajamas (oh, do I LOVE that one!).

- One of the most affordable and effective advertising platforms available—you can almost target down to their favorite shirt color.

- A quick way to check if your customers like you, or if there's a problem you're not yet aware of (trust me, if you're falling short, everyone will know about it. Best to catch it early!).

And there are many more perks, limited only by your imagination and creativity.

Now, writing just one chapter on social media is always a challenge. Usually you need a full book per platform to really get ahold of all the nuances, but I'll do my best in these few pages to create a general understanding, give you some tools, and then show you how to get the information you need to move forward. Fair enough?

The Dos and Don'ts of Social Media

Let's start with some social media dos and don'ts of social media in general, and then we'll drill down to platform specifics.

- **Be clear on your target audience** - If your target market is "everyone," your results will be "nothing". I know this has already been covered in the book, but it bears repeating.

- **Understand your target market's needs** - Make sure the need you want to be meeting is a need they've admitted to having.

- **Have a strategy** - The quickest and easiest way to understand how to put together a social media content plan is with the book The One Hour Content Plan by Meera Kothand, which you can find on Amazon at this link: http://bit.ly/socialstrategybook

- **Think "Living Room" or "Coffee Shop"** - Create a page where your ideal target market would hang out even if they weren't interested in buying.

- **Focus your content on these three ideas** - Educate, inspire, entertain.

- **Keep it short** - Everyone's in a hurry, so keep posts short. Once in a while, post something longer and meaningful (anywhere but Twitter!).

- **Ask questions** - Remember this is *social* media, so ask questions and start conversations.

- **Don't shout about your product** - You're not a hawker, you're an informed specialist. Craft worthy posts about your product, rather than "Buy Me" posts. Most of your posts should be about something other than what you're actually selling.

- **Be everywhere** - Be present on every platform, but just work one. I'll show you how to do that (without pulling your hair out) later in the chapter.

- **Before you post anything, ask yourself these two questions** - Is it likely that anyone would engage with this post? Who might "like," "comment," or "share" it?

- **Share your personality and life, but do not air your laundry** - Never post anything that will embarrass someone or make your followers feel uncomfortable.

- **Keep the names the same** - Don't have a different username for every platform. Before you set up your social media - or even your website - check here for something that works: http://bit.ly/CheckTheName

- **Use a professional headshot** - You want to look like you're serious about your business by having a professional profile picture. No hats, sunglasses, group photos, pictures of your cat... and nothing that looks like it came from a boudoir shoot (good grief, I've seen it all!).

- **Automate anything and everything you can** - If you're doing social media without automation, you're either spending too much time on social media and not enough time on your business, or you're not doing enough on social media to do any good.

- **Watch when you invite someone into your space** - Before you invite anyone to follow you on your business accounts, make sure you have about ten great and varied posts up there, so it looks interesting. Nothing like arriving to a new page and seeing nothing but the header and profile photo!

- **Watch *who* you invite into your space** - Don't invite all your friends, family, and pets to your business social media. Carefully seek out people who are actually in your target market and invite them. Social media platforms penalize pages where there a large number of followers but no activity. You need a targeted audience to get that necessary activity.

The Different Social Media Platforms

Before I go into detail here, know that the one constant with social media is that it changes. The platforms I'm discussing below are the biggest ones in the industry today. Tomorrow, one or more could be gone. I've also listed tools I've used and loved for years. They, too, could disappear at any time. If you need an alternative because of a major change, just ask.

Now, let's get down to brass tacks with each of the main platforms!

First, you need to know how and where to start.

I like to encourage people to be everywhere. While it's true that each platform has a somewhat specific audience (more men than women, younger rather than older, etc.) the truth is, there are always outliers. If you market using an automated scheduling program (Buffer, Hootsuite, etc.) you're able to be everywhere at once. This seriously boosts your SEO and allows people who are interested in engaging with you to use their favorite platform to do so.

You simply post everywhere (adjusting posts a little differently - mostly the hashtags - for the different platforms) and check into the ones that are less important to your business, less frequently, like twice a week instead of daily, for example. If the thought of being on "everywhere" is too much, you can always hire a social media team to help you create the allusion that you really are everywhere at all times

Facebook

Facebook's Audience[1]:

- 83% of women and 75% of men use Facebook.
- 83% of Facebook users worldwide are under the age of forty-five.
- 44% of Facebook users eighteen and older are women. 56% of users are men.
- 46.39% of Facebook users report being married, while another 39% report being single.
- As of January 2017, men ages eighteen to twenty-four make up the highest percentage of Facebook users by both age and gender, at 18%.

Getting Set Up:

- Set up a Facebook business page (http://bit.ly/FBBizSetUp). Why? Well, if you build your business on your personal profile rather than your business page, it's not only against Facebook's policy but:

  - You will be hindered by the number of followers you can have at any one time.

  - Having 800 followers on your personal page doesn't mean they're your target audience. Likely, very few of them care one whit about what you're selling. In fact, you're probably bothering most of them.

  - You have no way of telling how well you're communicating your message—are the right people responding?

  - You can't use any of the promotional tools Facebook has available to business owners.

---

1 These facts come from the article "75 Super-Useful Facebook Statistics for 2018" on Wordstream.com

How to Market on Facebook:

- Brands post an average of eight times per day on Facebook. You can get away with fewer posts, but two to three daily will likely be your minimum!
- Facebook is especially keen on video. A video created and uploaded directly to Facebook (rather than via YouTube or Vimeo, for example) gets a significant jump in visibility.

Twitter

Twitter's Audience[2]:

- 36% of Americans aged eighteen to twenty-nine years old use Twitter. Usage drops as age increases.
- 30% of Americans who earn $75,000 or more use Twitter.

Getting Set Up:

- Set up your Twitter account for your business by following the advice here: http://bit.ly/TwBizSetUp
- Use Twitter lists to keep on top of your best followers and industry experts.

How to Market on Twitter:

- Twitter moves quickly, so posting a minimum of five posts a day is recommended (don't faint— we'll get to that!).
- Find popular hashtags and see if you can work in your product or service around those.
- Two hashtags per post is ideal.

---

2 https://blog.hootsuite.com/twitter-statistics/

Google+

Google+'s Audience[3]:

- Nearly 74% of the audience is male.
- 72% of users are thirty-five or older.
- It is used by 40% of marketers as a social platform.

Getting Set Up:

- Google has a few moving parts that need to be set up correctly, or else you'll have to hire someone like me to untangle it. Untangling Google+ makes me cry, so here are the instructions for doing it right the first time: http://bit.ly/GPDoneRight

How to Market on Google+:

- It is recommended to post three times a day on Google+, and posting earlier rather than later in the day is recommended.
- Use an asterisk (the * symbol) at the beginning and end of your title so Google will bold it.
- Google+ users like substance, not fluff. Longer posts are fine here.
- Three hashtags per post is ideal.

Instagram

Important Facts[4]:

- Instagram has one-billion users, and there are 500 million daily users.
- People use Instagram as a way to follow their passions.
- 80% of users follow a business on Instagram.

---

3 http://www.statisticbrain.com/google-plus-demographics-statistics/

4 https://blog.hootsuite.com/instagram-statistics/

Instagram's Audience[5]:

- 80% of all Instagram users come from countries outside of the United States.
- It is used by 38% of women in the U.S. and 26% of men.
- Instagram's users are 38% women in the U.S. and 26% of men.
- 63 percent of thirteen to seventeen-year-olds use Instagram daily.

Getting Set Up:

- Here's how you set up Instagram for business success: http://bit.ly/InstBizSetUp

How to Market:

- Post one to two times per day, early in the morning and the wee hours of the night[6].
- Tell stories using Instagram Stories.
- Use video. Watching video has increased by more than 80% year-over-year[7] .

Pinterest

Pinterest's Audience[8]:

- 81% of Pinterest users are female.
- 40% of new signups are men; 60% are women.
- Men account for only 7% of total pins on Pinterest.
- Millennials use Pinterest as much as Instagram.
- Median age of a Pinterest user is forty; however, the majority of active pinners are below forty.

---

5 https://blog.hootsuite.com/instagram-statistics/

6 https://coschedule.com/blog/how-often-to-post-on-social-media/

7 https://business.instagram.com/blog/welcoming-two-million-advertisers/

8 https://www.omnicoreagency.com/pinterest-statistics/

Getting Set Up:

- Follow the instructions here for getting set up on Pinterest: http://bit.ly/PintBizSetUp

How to Market:

- If your audience is really active here, you are advised to post up to eleven times a day, but pull 80% of your posts from other boards. Otherwise, five times a day is recommended[9].
- Optimize your boards for Pinterest search because you want to make them easy to find!
- Make sure your images are striking!

LinkedIn

Important Facts:

- There are 500 million LinkedIn users.
- 40% people use LinkedIn daily.

LinkedIn's Audience10:

- 40 million students and recent college graduates are on LinkedIn.
- 57% are male users and 44% are female users.
- 13% of Millennia's (fifteen to thirty-four year olds) use LinkedIn.
- 28% of all male internet users use LinkedIn, whereas 27% of all female internet users do.
- 44% of LinkedIn users earn more than $75,000 a year.

---

9 https://coschedule.com/blog/how-often-to-post-on-social-media/

10 https://www.omnicoreagency.com/linkedin-statistics/

Getting Set Up:

- LinkedIn is a very different platform in many ways. You need to really invest some time in getting it set up properly. Here are some best practices for your LinkedIn profile: http://bit.ly/LIBizSetUp

How to Market:

- Post something daily that matters to business owners. Don't post anything that isn't going to grow someone's bottom line somehow. This is not Facebook.
- Share one update per day.
- Congratulate people on their achievements, birthdays, etc., under your announcement tab, this gets you in front of them. Use something original, not the automated reply.

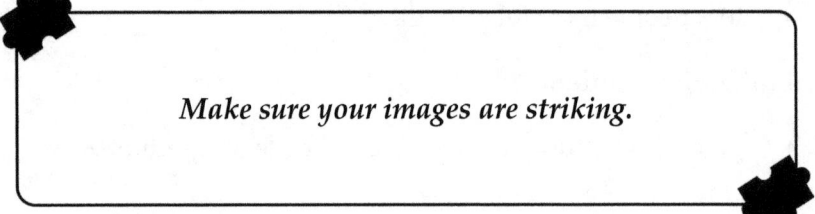

Make sure your images are striking.

Making It Work

Okay, let's talk about how to make this work. You have to have a system set up that helps you find/create posts quickly without too much effort, and you need to automate every step of the process that can justifiably be automated.

1. The first thing to create is a content calendar. You can use the one I use here (make a copy and save it to your computer):

http://bit.ly/HSPostTemplate. Plug in critical elements based on your content plan and then build around that.

a. Here's how it works with this sheet:

    i. **Quotes** - Fairly self-explanatory. Find great quotes by searching for multiple topics. I search "Quotes about social media," "Quotes about entrepreneurs," "Quotes about persevering," "Quotes about marketing," etc. Don't post a quote you've seen a hundred times.

    ii. **Fun Questions** - These are for creating a conversation started around a fun topic that has nothing to do with your business. "What's your favorite Starbucks drink?"; "What movie could you watch over and over again?"; "Where's your favorite holiday place?"; "What are you doing this weekend?"

    iii. **Did You Know** - This is a popular hashtag (#DYK) because people love trivia and interesting stats. These should be about your industry (not just your particular product/service).

    iv. **Biz Questions** - These are questions you ask regarding your business. In my case, I ask questions like, "Which is your favorite social media platform?"; "What's your social media pet peeve?"; "What's the funniest status update you've ever seen?"

    v. **Lifestyle Articles** - These are articles about things your followers are interested in that have almost nothing to do with your business. Again, in my case, I post quick recipes, articles about life balance, health and wellness, productivity, etc.

vi. **Business Articles** - These are about your topic. For me, they are articles about social media specifically, and business growth in general.

vii. **Inspirational** - These are posts that make people stand up taller—a video about someone who's overcome something, affirmations, a great business success story, etc. I would generally not use quotes here, as you'll already be posting quotes.

viii. **Tips** - These are short tips that are focused on your business. Use the length of a Twitter post (280 characters) as your guide. These should be quick, actionable takeaways.

ix. **Product** - Whatever you're trying to sell.

x. **Funny** - Anything that makes you laugh—a funny image, a puppy video, a joke, whatever you can find. Keep them clean unless your branding is all about being crass and edgy (surprisingly, some brands are!).

xi. **Special Days** - I get these from this site: www.daysoftheyear.com. Find anything that is either related to your business, or something that could create terrific conversation like "Sister's Day" on August 4th. You could get everyone to share a photo of themselves with their sisters.

xii. **Resources** - Have you found any books, apps, organizations, websites, etc., that are a great tool or resource for your ideal clients? Share a few different ones each month.

b. The highlighted sections above indicate that you should create your own images around these posts. The easiest way is to use pablo.Buffer.com which is dead easy and will post directly to your Buffer account. The next best one is www.Canva.com. Both are 100% free to use.

2. Create an account at www.Buffer.com so the posting of all of these posts can be automated according to a schedule you set up (you need the very affordable PRO account if you really want to save time).

3. Once you have this list created, you can use www.BulkBuffer.com to upload it them all at once to your Buffer account. You'll have to attach the photos manually, but the posts will all be automatically scheduled.

4. Buffer allows you to be everywhere as it posts to all of the above social channels, but once you have your posts up, you really only need to work the platform where your target market is. Check into the others every few days to respond to comments, but you don't have to actively build them all.

Another easy way to get posts up there is using www.PostPlanner.com (for a small fee), which pulls in the most popular items from the web. It also allows you to create a schedule—as you did in Buffer—and pull these in from PostPlanner. They are more limited in where they post (currently just Facebook, Twitter, and Instagram), but I like to go in here once a week and pull a lot of extra posts out for Twitter.

If all of this sounds overwhelming, you can:

1. Hire all of it out. I don't actually recommend this for small businesses, simply because who you are as a person is critical to your social media success. However, if you choose to do so, here are some questions to ask and topics to discuss with your potential social media manager:

a. Have them explain what they would do and why they would do it. What metrics do they track for results?

b. How would they handle a social media crisis (inappropriate posts, angry clients, etc.)?

c. What would their strategy be for growing your page?

d. Have them show you pages they manage and the results they've achieved.

2. Have some of it done for you. We offer two entry-level programs for this. One is custom (www.EffortlessSocialMedia.com), and one is based on industry (www.SocialMediaInABox.ca).

3. If you want to do this yourself, but need more detailed instructions, download my eBook *"10 Days to a Simple, Step-by-Step, Social Media System for Small Businesses"* on my website homepage here: www.hotspotsocialmedia.com/5YearBizGuide

My biggest tip would be just jump on! Start on a platform you're comfortable with, experiment and see what works, and then once it's up and running, add in the others through automation. It's amazing the kinds of people you meet on social media, and if you do it well, you'll never run out of warm leads for your business!

And don't forget to have fun!

CHAPTER 7

FINANCING THE BUSINESS

Now that you've got your plan in place, it's time to talk about financing your business and getting the money you need to get off the ground.

You only have one opportunity to make a first impression with a bank or investor. Their decision to loan you money or invest in your company will be based on this impression—how you present yourself to them, the confidence they have in your business, and how you are going to be able to pay them back or make them money.

To start, you will need to create a business plan as outlined in Chapter 3. This chapter will focus on the numbers that you will need to put together for the business plan.

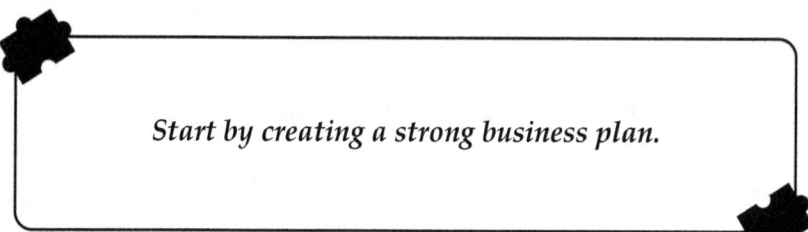

Start by creating a strong business plan.

How Much Money Do You Need?

Let's start with looking at the three basic numbers every business owner should know.

Cost of goods sold, cost of services sold or direct costs – These numbers are the costs associated to produce your product or service. The best way to describe it is if you didn't have any clients buying your product or service, you would not have to incur the cost.

You wouldn't have to rent a screen and projector if your event wasn't happening, correct? You wouldn't even have to buy the coffee and food for the event if it was not going to take place in the first place. Or, if you are a printing company, you would not need to buy ink if there were no clients to print for. A photographer would not have printing costs, an artist would not need to buy paint, and a massage therapist would not need massage oil if their clients did not exist or their services were not needed. These are all examples of direct costs associated with the cost of doing business.

Operating expenses – These are costs that you need to spend regardless of whether you have clients or not. As an example, if you pay monthly rent for your office or shop space, this would still be an expense whether you have clients or not. Typically, this cost also includes administrative costs, offices supplies, insurance, and memberships to other associations or groups.

Income or revenue – This is the amount of money you received in return for your product or service. Note that this does not include any taxes you may have collected in the process. Taxes need to be separately tracked to remit back to the government.

For the purpose of financing, they want to also know all your sources of income, including if you have a job and how much it is contributing to your household.

Banks or investors typically want to see this information in a table showing the trend over time on a monthly basis. This table will not only show the history of the business as well as seasonal fluctuations, it will also show a projection into the future. The past will tell the bank how successful your business has been or not been. The future projection will show how successful you can be based on a % increase per year. It also shows the bank your ability to pay back the loan.

If you are still in the startup phase of your business and don't have a financial history, it is perfectly acceptable to take your best guess. Your guess should be realistic based on research from vendors. Write out all your assumptions, so they can see how you came up with the numbers. This research will show how serious you are about your business.

Based on the information you put together, you can then determine how much money you need. Everyone's situation is different, so there are no set rules that need to be followed here.

Qualifying for Financing

The banks are mostly concerned with your ability to pay them back. In order for them to feel confident you can pay them back, they will look at the past history of both you personally and that of your business and the amount of your current debt. They will then assess your risk to them. Your personal and business past is usually an indicator of how you will perform in the future. If you don't have much of a business history, then they will probably look at your personal credit history.

If you have a full or part-time job on the side, this is probably the best time to ask for a loan. Banks like to loan people money when they don't need it. It is usually harder to get approval when you are desperate for the funds.

If you have a bad credit rating, they will look at how long ago it was and what the situation was. Bottom line: it will be harder for you to get financing with bad credit, but it's not necessarily impossible. All it really means is that you will be considered high-risk and may have to pay higher interest rates.

As a business owner, it is to your benefit to be responsible in the management of your finances. You never know if in the future you may want to expand your business and grow. This will keep your doors open in the future for financing.

Financing Options

Before looking at traditional financing options and heading to the bank, you should consider researching to see if there are government grants available to help your small business startup.

A grant is a sum of money given to a business for a certain purpose when the business meets a specific set of criteria. There are people you can hire to help investigate this area to find any and all possible grants that you and your business may qualify for.

Another avenue to look at before going to the bank is to get a loan from friends or family. They might be able to get you out of a temporary rut if that is all you need. It is good to pay these people back as soon as possible since you never know if you might need their help again in the future.

If the amount of financing you require is low, most banks will start you off with a simple business credit card. This will also help you build a credit rating for your business.

A bank may also offer you a line of credit. This is a fixed pre-approved amount that you can draw cash from when you need it. You can pay it back with interest as quickly or as slowly as you want. It's like a mini pre-approved loan.

Lines of credit can be secured or unsecured depending on your situation. When I was young and didn't have much of a credit rating, I took $5000 and gave it to the bank as security towards a $5000 line of credit. This is a 100% secured line of credit. As my credit rating improved over time, the banks now give me a line of credit that is unsecured.

Another way to get a secured line of credit is to use the house that you own as security. The amount will be based on what you and your bank agree upon. Keep in mind that if you cannot pay back the line of credit, the bank may take whatever security you used to get their money back.

The next level of financing is to get a bank loan. This is typically for larger amounts based on a fixed interest rates and terms.

Todd Purcell, a commercial loans broker with CFO to Go Canada, says, "Banks are fairly simple to understand. You simply need to fit in their box, and they will work with you. The hard part is fitting into their box when you are a new business owner. You should set a goal and plan to fit into this box."

So, what are the banks looking for?

Todd shares the three main areas that banks look at:

- Good Credit History
- Positive Net Worth
- Revenue

If you have all of the above, excellent! You can be approved for financing from the bank.

If your credit is strong, then the amount of financing you may receive from the bank will depend largely on how high your net worth is, how much revenue you bring in, and if they believe you can service the debt based on their guidelines (not yours!).

Here are some tips that Todd shares about how to improve your chances for financing:

1. **Be the First Investor**

   The first question any banker or savvy investor will ask is, "How much have you invested?" If you cannot answer this question, and eventually prove it, you are less likely to get the financing you need. Depending on the type of financing you are seeking, a rule of thumb is to be prepared to invest 10% to 25% of the total funds required to launch your business and sustain it.

2. **Begin Planning Early**

   Planning early does not just include your business plan, it also includes preparing yourself early to be able to start this new venture. The amount of early planning required will be different for everyone; however, the two most important factors are:

   - **Check your credit** - For a startup business with no financial history, good credit may not be enough. Aim for

Excellent credit. If you are familiar with credit scores, a score of 700 should be your minimum goal.

- **Save money** (or have access to money) – This includes your initial investment plus enough to cover your personal bills for 6 to 12 months. If you have a spouse that can cover the household bills, let the bank know, as this eliminates a lot of their risk.

3. Plan for the Unexpected

No matter how much you plan and prepare, there are always circumstances that arise that you could not have seen coming. Be sure that when you build your business plan and financial plan, you have a strategy to handle the unexpected, and that you have some funds set aside for it.

4. Be Financially Positive

Starting a business requires a huge amount of positivity, and the banks expect no less when it comes to your finances. Having a strong net worth shows that you can manage your finances, set aside money, and plan for the future.

5. Know Your Numbers

The banks typically do not care if you plan to make $50,000 or $1,000,000 in your first year. What they care about is that you know how much you plan to make, what it will cost, and that there is enough money left over in your plan to pay them back. If you do not know how much your product will cost, how much you intend to sell it for, and how much you will make from a sale, keep planning until you have the answers, or find someone to help you get the answers.

6. Know What You Need

"What is the money being used for?" is possibly the second most common question asked by banks and investors. They want to know if you are purchasing equipment, doing leasehold improvements, hiring staff, or need funds to manage your day-to-day operations (working capital). They also want to know if you are taking their money to pay yourself a salary. Business loans are not income for the business owner; they are an investment to grow the business so that it may generate more income.

This is why in your pre-planning, you need to set aside funds to cover your personal bills or have a spouse with an income to cover it.

7. Have Revenue

This may not be possible if you are a startup. However, the banks favor businesses with revenue. If you can have some pre-sales made, or perhaps you tested out your business part-time prior to deciding to go full-time into business for yourself, it can improve your chances of getting the financing you desire.

8. Offer Security

It is safe to assume that you will be giving personal guarantees on every business loan you receive. This offers the bank some peace of mind that you will not run away with their money or bankrupt the company. The more security you can offer, the more likely you will be approved for a loan. Real estate is the bank's favorite asset for security, while vehicles, jewelry and other household goods do not offer much security. One commonly overlooked asset, however, is the cash/investment account linked to whole life and universal life insurance policies. If you have been paying into one of these types of permanent life insurance for a number of years, you may have a substantial cash value, which can be used as security for loans at some of the lowest rates on the market.

9. <u>Know a Good Offer</u>

In the early stages of your business, you may not receive the full amount of funding you request from a bank or lender, or perhaps the rate is higher than you had planned. It does not mean it is not a good offer. As a startup, receiving an offer from the bank or lender that is not what you wanted, is their way of offering you an olive branch. The bank is saying that they believe in your business, and they want you to get started and prove to them that you can do what you said in your plan. Then you can go back and ask for more.

10. <u>Build Relationships</u>

A good account manager at the bank can be a huge asset to your business. If you keep them informed and have good communication, they can go to bat for you and get you approved for loans that you may not have received without that relationship. They want to see your business succeed because no bank wants bad accounts. Therefore, look for a a broker who can introduce you to some great account managers. It is also good to build relationships with at least two banks. You never know what may happen in the future, and having a back-up bank that knows you, can make the difference during tougher times.

These are great tips from Todd Purcell, with CFO to Go Canada, to improve your chances to get your loan approved. Todd works with small and mid-sized companies looking for financing to start or grow their business.

If you cannot get approval from a financial institution, you can consider finding someone to invest in your business. There are pro's and con's to having an investor depending on the terms of the agreement:

- **Con** – You may lose a percentage of your business to your investor.

- **Con** – You may lose some control of your business; the investor might want you to make changes that you don't want to make.

- **Pro** – You can get the funds quickly.

- **Pro** – You can get access to the business expertise of the investor to help your business.

Crowdfunding is another great option for fundraising the funds you need. This can be very effective if you have a very interesting business idea that is unique and that also appeals to the general public. An additional benefit of Crowdfunding, is it can be used as a marketing resource to pre-sell your product and or service prior to your grand opening!

Getting Help

There is a great deal that you need to know about getting financing.

Since you only have that one opportunity to make a good first impression with the bank, it is advisable to speak to someone who is knowledgeable in this area. Start by creating a strong business plan. You might need to ask your accountant to help value the assets associated with your business, especially if you have equipment or inventory.

Also, there are people who specialize in working with businesses looking for financing, like Todd Purcell, with CFO to Go Canada. He is like a broker that can shop around for you and guide you through the process. He will know which banks you have the best chance at getting approved for financing according to your specific and unique situation.

Make sure you have a clear understanding of any agreement you may enter into. If you don't understand something, ask first. You don't want to blindly sign a contract without fully knowing the terms and conditions.

Download your free guide to
writing a business plan for the bank
www.cfo2gocanada.com/5YearBizGuide

CHAPTER 8

THE FOUNDATION FOR YOUR BUSINESS

Securing funding through an investor or bank may be quite the overwhelming task in the beginning, but having a foundation for your business will help create less stress and more stability regardless of what you're facing in the financial department.

One day you will wake up and realize that your business is building so much momentum, that you can't keep up on your own. You may be overwhelmed with the amount of administrative work associated with running a business—perhaps marketing and social media are taking up a lot of your time, and you are starting to drown to keep your clients happy.

Your SOS message may be going out screaming, "Help!"

Or, if you are a glass half full kind of person, congratulations! You are now entering the next stage of running a business!

You are growing.

This, my friend, is what business owners aim for. It's time to seriously start looking at the foundation of your business and how it can to help you grow.

Every house has a foundation or basement for the building to sit on. This represents the core for all businesses. It includes accounting, legal, building a team, computer systems, etc. These are the basics that every business needs to run smoothly and efficiently.

Let's now look at the walls of the house. They represent your operations—how you plan to deliver your product or service to your clients. These would be your services that are available online, mobile, in a retail store, etc. Everyone's business is unique, so that is what makes everyone's "house" different.

Lastly, we have the paint on the house. This is the sales and marketing of your business and what makes your house (or business) look appealing and attractive.

Have you ever run across someone who was in a hurry to sell their house, but they didn't have time or money to make the necessary repairs to the house to cover up the cracks?

What do those people always do? Most will paint the house to make it look good in hopes that the prospective buyers won't notice the cracks in the house.

You don't want to be doing this for your business.

You can implement an aggressive sales and marketing strategy to get a plethora of clients. If you cannot properly deliver to the increased demand for your product, you could find yourself in a heap of trouble. Having unhappy clients and doing damage control is not a good place you want to be.

One person even told me they got so overwhelmed that they shut their doors and closed the business down! This is why planning for managed growth is so important.

Spending Time in the Right Places

Let's start with getting you some help.

Before you can do that, you need to figure out what you need help with. This is when you have to figure out where you are spending your time. Are you doing the right things to grow your business, or are you working on mundane repetitive tasks or doing things that you hate doing that someone else can help you with?

Many people can hazard a guess at where they are spending their time. When they actually track the hours for a week or two, they are typically amazed at the results. They realize they are spending more time on menial tasks than they are spending on the ones that will move their business forward.

If your time is worth $100 per hour, why would you want to do something when you can pay someone $50 per hour to do it? Sure, you can save $50, but you could have spent that hour bringing in more money into your business. Instead, you lost that time and that potential money.

There is a saying that says you should be working "on" your business instead of "in" your business. When remembered and utilized appropriately, this saying can be quite beneficial to any business and business owner.

Working "in" your business means doing what is required now—like invoicing, filing, accounting, etc. Working "on" your business is working on tasks that will bring you more business in the future. It could be planning the next marketing campaign or evaluating a new CRM system to track your clients.

To figure out where you are spending your time, you need to record what you are doing for your business for a week or two. The longer you track your time, the more you will understand where you may have issues and course correct sooner than later. You will know whether you are spending your time in the right places. They say when you are a startup, over 50% of your time should be in sales and marketing activities.

You can write down the time you are spending on different activities on a piece of paper or journal. Or, you can record it on a spreadsheet or download a time tracking application.

It doesn't really matter which method you choose as long as it works for you, *and* you remember to use it. If you keep forgetting to record your time, try a different method. The data you gather will be very valuable for making decisions in the future.

> *Where and how you are spending your time is just as important as knowing how you are spending your money in your business. Start to track it to see what you are doing.*

When tracking your time, you should put things into different categories. Here are some examples that may apply to you:

- **Accounting** – Time spent on organizing receipts, entering the information into a tracking system, invoicing clients, collecting payment, paying bills, and anything else related to your financials.

- **Sales and marketing** – This includes networking events, your time on social media, talking to prospective clients, creating proposals, following up with clients and anything else related to bringing in new clients.

- **Delivering the product** – If your business is service-based, this is the time you spend on delivering the service to your clients and getting paid.

- **Operations** – These are activities related to your operations. This could include making purchases for your business, negotiating with vendors, troubleshooting problems, dealing with employees, training new hires, implementing automation tools and anything else related to running the business.

- **Research and development** – This is the time spent to create new products or services. This could include the development of a new workshop or program or researching the potential of adding new products

- **Personal** – If you track the amount of time you spent on personal activities vs business, it will give you an idea of what percentage of your time is business vs personal. This helps to make sure you have a good work-life balance.

Once you know where you spend most of your time, you can then decide whether you need to readjust your priorities, automate your processes, and/or hire someone to help.

Creating Systems

Before you can start looking at automating your workflows or even think about hiring someone, you need to have systems in place first!

Many people say that they don't have systems in place when, in reality, they probably do. When asked what they do with their receipts, some may say, "I put them in a shoebox and take them to the accountant at the end of the year." This isn't exactly the best way to handle receipts, but it is definitely one workflow. There is no right or wrong workflow; just some that are more efficient than others! The goal is to improve the system and see how it can be automated.

If you have well-defined systems, make sure you document the workflow. Having it written down does not mean it is cast in stone. It just means this is the way you do things today. As your business grows and changes, your workflows may need to be modified to adapt to the changing conditions.

Documented workflows will help with automation and training new people you bring on board. When you get really big, these workflows can be used to open a second location or move into a franchising model. Remember you start small, but think big.

Automation

The biggest problem with automating some of your repetitive processes is that there is a large number of software applications out there which can do similar things. There are too many choices out there when it comes to automating invoicing systems, tracking receipts, managing clients' workflow and many more to accurately choose one without testing it first.

I once asked a group of people for CRM recommendations, and within fifteen minutes, I had a list of twelve! I don't have time to research all twelve, and I am sure in the end, they all do very similar things, just in a different way. The issue is I can learn whatever system you put in front of me, so there is a good chance I may go with the first one. Researching applications is very time consuming.

The best way to automate processes is to start with working with someone who is good with creating workflows. Once these are in place, you can bring in an automation specialist to put together a solution that works for you.

There is a cost associated with all automation projects. You should think about the time and stress it will save you as a result of the investment.

The first process I automated in my business was my appointment booking system.

Something this simple saved me time from going back and forth trying to find a date that worked with both parties. Plus, to reduce the number of cancellations or forgotten appointments, I was sending a reminder email twenty-four hours before the meeting to confirm the meeting details. By having this whole process automated, I was able to spend more time working on other things that make a difference to grow my business.

If you're ready to create more systems and processes in your business, now is the time!

Remember you start small, but think big.

Getting Help

Not everything can be automated, and sometimes you may prefer a personal touch but lack the time to actually do it. If that is the case, you should consider getting someone to help you.

If you decide to hire someone, put together a list of the tasks that can easily be handed off to someone. Review your workflow to see which tasks must be done by you and what can be handed off.

These would be repetitive tasks that do not require extensive technical knowledge, and you can easily train someone else. Usually the first person a business owner hires is an assistant to take care of administrative duties and then maybe a bookkeeper.

The list of tasks you put together will need to be put into a job description. People will want to know what they are expected to do. You also have to have a good idea of what background this person should have, and how much you are willing to pay them.

When you are making your first hire and still growing your income, you may not be able to afford to hire someone full-time or even commit to part-time hours. If you commit to the number of hours per week, then you must pay them regardless of whether you have work for them to do or not.

A good way to transition into getting the help you need in your business is to use the services of a contractor. These assistants would have a number of clients they service, and you only pay them for the work they do for you. They are usually experienced in a number of different areas and may even be able to do things faster than you. Not all people are familiar with putting together PowerPoint presentations, but an experienced administrative professional may be able to get the work done in a shorter period of time for you.

By using the services of a contractor, you may end up paying a higher hourly rate for their services. It is pay as you go, and you won't have to worry about the additional burden that comes with hiring an employee. An employee means you must adhere to all the rules associated with local labor practices.

In Canada, when hiring a consultant or sub-contractor, you don't need to follow the employee guidelines. To do this legitimately, however, you cannot be their only client and they must have the flexibility to set their own hours and work terms. If you are the contractor's only client, then the Canadian government says the contractor is actually an employee and you need to follow employee rules. As each scenario is different, consult your accountant.

When hiring a contractor, you should put together some type of working agreement. At a minimum, it should include the description of service, hourly rates, working terms, a confidentiality agreement, and how to exit the agreement. Each business is different, so you may want consult with a lawyer. Keep in mind your contractor will know all the inner working of your business, so you should make sure what you have created doesn't get stolen.

There will come a day when you realize the amount of money you are paying your contractor and the hours they are working is constantly high. This means you have enough work to hire a full-time employee. When you are ready to hire, consider getting a bookkeeper or accountant to help you set this up. They will be able to help you with the cost justification as the cost of an employee is more than just their salary. You need to incorporate vacation days, taxes and possible health, dental, and retirement benefits.

Many business owners will say "It's faster to do it myself!". Yes it is. But that's not the point.

The goal is to free up your time. Yes it will take you longer up front to train the person or to get the automation set up. And yes, you won't see the results right away. You will, however, eventually see the benefits when it's completely handed over.

Consider it as an investment into your future sanity!

Building a Team

Your team is not only the people you hire. It's also your contractors, vendors, coaches, mentors, family and friends. They are the people you surround yourself with every day that are there to support you on your journey.

Your team can make you or break you. Choose your team members carefully. They will represent your company in front of the clients, and it's your reputation on the line.

Each time you hire someone that is not a good fit with your business, it will cost you money to deal with it later. Think of it like entering into a marriage. Not only is the cost of divorce high, but the emotional impact is stressful. It's the same way in business.

When choosing to bring someone onboard, look at the skills they can bring to the table and their strengths and weaknesses. Also, do their core values align with yours? Someone who is a perfectionist is not a good fit with someone who is always trying to cut corners.

Your team will represent your company when they are in front of your clients. You should outline what your customer care goals are, and what your expectations are. This needs to be communicated to your team so everyone knows what the ultimate goals are.

When you find someone who is really good, pay and treat them well. There is a better chance that they will stay longer and be devoted to helping you and your business flourish. Each time you have someone leave your company, it costs you time and money to find someone new and train that person. They may interview well, but there is always a risk that they are not a good personality fit with your business; therefore, you might have to go through the process again.

If you can't afford to pay a high wage, then consider compensating a person some other way. Sometimes what's more important than the money is the ability to have flexible work hours, so they can be home for their kids after school. Or it's getting experience in a new area, or working from home. Find out what is important to them and create something that benefits everyone.

In the end, you want to create an environment in your company where everyone is there because they *want* to be there. People are more effective when they are doing something they love with people they like. Ruling by dictatorship and "because I said so" doesn't inspire or motivate people. They need a sense of belonging.

Make your environment fun, motivational, and respectful. We all spend a lot of time at work, so make it positive and purposeful. Keep the lines of communication open and make work a safe place to be. It's a team effort. Put all this in place and the business should thrive.

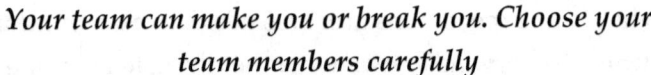

Your team can make you or break you. Choose your team members carefully

CHAPTER 9

MAKING MORE PROFIT

One of the most common reasons why businesses fail is due to the lack of cash flow, meaning there is not enough money to pay the bills at the end of the month. How can that be when there is money coming in? The key to not getting into trouble is knowing and understanding your numbers.

Most people don't have unlimited time and money. Knowing your numbers will allow you to control your business instead of having your business control you. You should make decisions based on fact and not on what your gut is telling you. Trends in your numbers will allow you to be *proactive* with your business as opposed to *reactive*. The sooner you take control of your numbers, the sooner you can make more profit.

If you don't follow the steps in this chapter, you can still make money and be successful. By knowing your numbers, you can make more money in a shorter period of time.

Here are some common questions your numbers will help answer:

- Why you don't have enough money to pay bills at the end of the month?
- What can you afford to buy?
- How can you pay for large purchases?

- How can you manage your money when you have seasonal income?
- How you can make more money without increasing your prices?
- Are you pricing your product properly?
- How can you pay yourself more?

Data is only useful if it is presented in a manner where it can become knowledge. It is knowledge that allows businesses owners to decipher what is going on in their business and make appropriate decisions.

Who can help?

Before digging into the numbers, let's explore the people who may be involved with your numbers and make sure everyone is on the same page as to their roles in the process.

Bookkeeper - They enter the accounting data into a system that is used to track income and expenses for a business. Some business owners do this on their own by using either the good old-fashioned method of pencil and paper, or manually entering it into a spreadsheet or accounting program. With advancements in technology, you can even take a photo of your receipts and the program takes care of the rest.

A typical bookkeeper will enter your numbers and send you a regular monthly report. At the end of the year, the bookkeeper will give you a report on how your business is doing by creating the appropriate yearly statements and also submitting the proper documentation to your accountant for tax purposes. A bookkeeper may also help you calculate payroll for your employees, pay your bills, and collect on outstanding invoices.

For many business owners, this is a dreaded task and is one of the first things that gets handed off to someone else to do. They may leave it in the shoebox until it's time to take it to the accountant for taxes at the end of the year. This method is prone to the business owner getting into financial trouble.

"By getting a bookkeeper, you will free up your time to work on growing your business, instead of doing mundane administrative tasks," says Tina Saini of High Power Solutions Accounting. "As your business grows, you don't want to be burdened with the tracking of the money"

Accountant - An accountant is different than a bookkeeper, in that they will take the information compiled by the bookkeeper and look at it in different ways. Some accountants also offer bookkeeping services, so they become a one-stop shop.

Note that all accountants are not created equal. They can be trained in different areas of accounting, so they may not be specialized in the area you are looking for. The following describes the ones a startup or small business owner may need. Larger corporations have other accounting needs that is not covered in this book.

- **Tax accountant** – Specializes in helping you reduce taxes for both your personal and business.

- **Operational accounting** – Specializes in understanding how to make a business more profitable. If a business is not doing well, this type of accountant can help you with situational analysis to understand what can be changed to improve the financial health of your business.

- **Business valuation** – Specializes in understanding the value of a business. This is helpful when buying or selling a business. When buying a business, you should have a good understanding of how the business is doing. It might look good on paper, but a professional accountant trained in this area may uncover skeletons in their closet. When selling, the accountant can tell you how much your business is worth and what it could sell for. They might be able to even tell you what to change to improve the value of the business to make it more attractive to sell at a higher price.

Make sure you understand what your accountant's specialty is.

"A bookkeeper takes care of you month to month whereas an accountant looks after you year to year," says Tina Saini of High Power Solutions Accounting. "An accountant can also help you deal with any government interactions from reporting to audits. This process can be very daunting, which is why an accountant can alleviate the stress with understanding the system."

Tina reminds us that, "At some point you have to let go and learn to trust other people to handle some part of the business."

**Download interview questions when
hiring a bookkeeper or accountant at
www.highpowersolutions.ca/5YearBizGuide**

Operations Manager - The operations manager has a different view of the world with the mandate to make more profit. In a startup company or small business, the business owner takes on the role of operations manager.

To achieve efficiency and profitability goals, there are distinctive areas of the operations that need to be reviewed for continual improvement:

- **Operational workflows** – Find ways to do things faster and better. If the ultimate goal is to complete the job and invoice it to the client, is there something that can be done at the beginning of the workflow that will improve the invoicing process at the end? Perhaps it's integrating the ordering or quote system with the invoicing system so people are not entering the same information multiple times.

- **Production** – Tracking time and costs associated with your product or service. This will help determine whether you are properly priced and allows you to improve your operational efficiencies. Doing things faster and better is always the ultimate goal!

- **The team** – Having the right people in the proper roles and making sure everyone is motivated to work at their peak performance.

- **Financials** - Understanding what the numbers are and how to improve the operations.

When choosing someone to help you in any of these three roles, you need to find someone you trust. You will be exposing all of your financials—good and bad—to these people. You will be vulnerable while sharing your most intimate personal financial world to them. Interview a few people, learn along the way, and choose the one that you are most comfortable with.

What are the Numbers?

To make effective decisions, you should look at both the accounting and production numbers.

The accounting numbers come from all the information that is entered into the accounting system. Data is only helpful if it is in a format that is useful to answer whatever question you may have with your business.

When I first started receiving the monthly financial statements for the business, I really wasn't sure what to do with the reports or what they were telling me.

Sure, they were showing how much I made and spent in a given month, but I didn't understand how to make that information helpful to me in the business.

Being the Excel Queen that I am, I locked myself in the office and started creating a spreadsheet. I emerged with a work of art! It showed me trends and patterns, and over time, it actually predicted what the upcoming year would be. I was able to better plan how my resources were being used and how to invest into the future.

Here is a sample of what you can uncover from your accounting numbers:

- **Income from product lines** – Determine which products are bringing in the most income and which are most profitable. Those that are not selling well may be removed in the upcoming year.

- **Reducing expenses** – Find out where you are spending your money and whether there are ways to reduce costs. If 20% of your expenses are going towards interest on your credit card bill, consider calling your credit card company to see if they can maybe reduce the interest rate or come up with a better payment plan.

- **Client information** – Find out who your top clients are and profile them, so you can focus your marketing efforts towards that demographics. Also, if over 50% of your income is coming from one client, then you could be in trouble if that client leaves. You want your income to be better balanced.

- **General operating expense** – This is the cost to run your business if you had no clients. This could be items like software, insurance, rent, etc. Are there items you can reduce or remove that won't make much of a difference?

- **Analyzing your cash flow** – This will help you manage paying your bills every month and tell you whether you can afford to make large purchases. It will also help you make future projections. If you are trying to get financing for your business, you will need this information.

- **Gross margin** - This number tells you how much money you make for every dollar you sell. 20% gross margin means you will make $0.20 for every $1 you sell.

Accounting is not the only place where you can gather numbers to help you make decisions for your business. The numbers you get from your production is also a wealth of information. Since all businesses are different, here are just a few things that can be tracked:

- **Time spent on activities** – This will ensure you are spending time in the right places to grow your business. You can re-prioritize your time based on the results. When you combine the time you spend on sales and marketing activities with your marketing expenses, this will tell you your cost of acquisition which is the amount of money you spend to get one new client.

- **Time spent on projects** – This is very helpful if you are creating packages and quoting a fixed price for services.

- **Marketing effectiveness** – This determines which marketing activities are giving you the best return on your investment

- **Track time and costs to create your product** – This allows you to improve your profit by tracking efficiency improvements in your process that will allow you to manage your costs.

- **Employee performance** – This can be used to track continual process improvement.

- **Mileage tracking** – Combined with tracking your time to drive, you will see the true cost of providing mobile services.

How to Get the Numbers You Need

It's all fine to understand what your numbers can be used for, but now you have to put together a system to get the information in your hands.

To do that, you must first be committed to the process. Without this commitment, you will still be running your business based on your gut instincts rather than facts.

To get to these magical numbers, here are the steps:

Collect the Data – The more detailed you get when collecting the data, the better your analysis will be. For example, it is fine to know you spend on average $700 for advertising, but it would be nice to know out of those advertising dollars how much was spent on networking events, websites or media. For this reason, you should plan what you want your categories to be.

For collecting accounting data, you can either use an accounting program or, if you don't have a lot of transactions, a simple spreadsheet will do. With technology today, some apps even allow you take a picture of your receipts and enter them into the system. Manual paper methods are not recommended, as it will be cumbersome to do repetitive calculations for the analysis portion.

For collecting production data, the majority will come from time tracking and combining the results with your accounting data. People naturally hate time tracking, but it can provide you a wealth of information. Time tracking can either be done using a spreadsheet or a time tracking app that you find online. There are other things that can be collected as production data, but it will be dependent on your business and will be customized to you.

When using online applications, you should look for ones that allow you to export the data into an Excel or CSV format. Many will have built in reports and will do some analysis for you, but this is not usually enough, especially if you are combining accounting with production data.

Analyzing the Data – Now that you have collected the data, it's time to look and see the trends associated it. This includes looking at changes over time, percentages, and averages. There are many ways to analyze your data, and this will solely depend on your business.

The easiest way to do the analysis is to use a spreadsheet program. This allows you to look at your data in a number of different angles. As long as the app you are using to collect the data allows for an export into Excel, you can slice and dice your data in a number of different ways.

You are not alone if you are cringing at the words "Excel" and "spreadsheets". The tricky part is finding someone who is good at doing this analysis for you.

Some bookkeepers and accountants may be able to help you, but many only focus on the accounting numbers and may not want to help you incorporate the production side. Your mentors or coaches may be able to refer you to someone for help.

Key to Success

Now that you know how knowing your numbers can help you make a profit, and what you need to put in place to make it happen, here are some tips to make this process a success:

- **Make a commitment and have the disciple to stick to it** – You can still make money without knowing your numbers. This commitment will allow you to make *more* money *faster*.

- **Create a system that works for you** – If it's not working, then change it until it becomes an easy system for you to follow. Remember, there is no right or wrong way to do something — it's just that some ways are more efficient than others.

- **Get into a habit** – It takes 6 weeks to create a new habit. Don't stop the system until it becomes a habit.

- **Be consistent** – This could be how you enter the data. If you decide web services are an advertising cost, and one time you accidentally put it in as an office expense, your numbers will not be accurate anymore. Or if you start using one method to collect the data, then if you change it down the road, it will be an effort to move it to the new system.

- **Ask for help** – If you are not sure what you are doing in this area, find someone that can get you started.

I find that many business owners understand the need to know the numbers, but they often become overwhelmed and don't know where to start. This was the main motivating factor for me to create the **Magic in the Numbers program** — giving business owners the customized tools and training to easily access this information.

Planning for Wealth

I have one final note about your numbers that I think is extremely important and crucial to your overall, long-term success. One day you will wake up and realize that the balance in your bank account is growing more than you expected. Your income will greatly exceed your expenses.

This is a good place to be.

Here are some options for you:

- **Re-invest** – Put money back into your company and expand your business.

- **Pay yourself more** – Remember, this means you may end up paying more taxes.

- **Invest into other sources** – This should be done with a wealth advisor that specializes in helping business owners plan their investment growth within a company. A good advisor will help you minimize the taxes you pay and protect and grow your assets for retirement.

The ultimate dream for a business owner is to have enough money to retire and enjoy life and family time. Your expertise is what you deliver to your clients. Focus your time to grow your business and reach your dream. Find experts to help you in these other areas to help you along the way.

**Download the calculator to find out how much money you need to save for retirement to maintain your current lifestyle
www.highpowersolutions.ca/5YearBizGuide**

Tina Saini of High Power Solutions Accounting reminds us about this. "You work hard to build your company, it is important to maintain your current lifestyle and financial independence into the future."

CHAPTER 10

EXPERT CHAPTER CONTRIBUTOR

Marion Skaja,
Barrister & Solicitor

Marion Skaja loves working with small business owners – the passionate, ‚in over their heads' committed adventurers who need a little pointing in the right direction before they get into trouble – you don't know what you don't know until it sees you in court.

CHAPTER 10

THE ART OF HERDING CATS - PREVENTIVE LAW FOR STARTUPS

The statistics for successful startup businesses are dismal. As Nicki already mentioned, most fail within the first five years. All those hard working, visionary, adventurous and entrepreneurial types who risk and lose it all—gone in a puff of well-intentioned smoke.

The social, financial, and often familial fallout is palpable, with many losing their shirts, their spouses, and their friends as a result of borrowed money never returned, aspiring dreams never fulfilled, and too many years of intense financial stress on the family while trying to right the sinking ship.

It doesn't have to be that way, however. The good news is that a good deal of these financial disasters are self-inflicted and could have been prevented by good old-fashioned advice *before* setting out on the entrepreneurial road leading to much hoped for success and high reward.

As in many things, solid relationships are the foundation of success. The entrepreneur has to wear many hats in the startup phase— sometimes for many years—often having great knowledge about the product or service offering but little financial, management, or legal know-how.

And there are always few financial resources that need to be spread among many different areas of the business that scream for priority status over the rest.

Nevertheless, the wise entrepreneur will understand that good advice is the most precious resource available and will seek out the right people from the very beginning, to accompany the startup on its journey to a well-prepared, well-designed, successful, and sustainable business that will beat the odds.

It goes without saying that the best time to find a lawyer you like, feel confident with, and trust, is NOT during a crisis at 4:54 pm on a Friday before a long weekend.

Yet, business crises have a habit of striking at unusual times and do not tend to keep "banker's hours". An organized entrepreneur will have researched, interviewed, and chosen a well-established lawyer long before that inevitable crisis hits.

As an entrepreneur myself, and as a lawyer who is passionate about the successful dreams of entrepreneurs greatly benefiting society, I believe the following tips will provide startups just like yours with insight into the many ways their business can benefit from sound, practical advice sought and heeded long before unnecessary disaster strikes.

Please note that given the scope of this chapter and the wide variety of types of businesses, entrepreneurial challenges, and local jurisdictions of the likely readership of this book, I have kept this discussion fairly general. I make no claim to pointing out every challenge or legal risk that your startup may face in the future.

This contribution is not to be taken as legal advice that will protect your startup from all legal liability, but instead should provide an understanding of the often-misunderstood value of directly consulting and building a great relationship with a lawyer whom you know will have your back through the entrepreneurial life's endlessly exciting ups and downs.

Lawyers are people, too, and irrespective of the tired lawyer jokes, generally very much enjoy partnering with and assisting entrepreneurs as they progress from startup to successful sustainable business. We admire your courage, passion and commitment and want to be part of and create your positive journey.

Eight "CATS" For Successful Startups to Herd from the Start

Legal liability comes in many forms for the entrepreneur. Much of it arises from legislation and contracts, while some arise from torts (a wrongful act or omission that grounds a civil claim) or a criminal act or omission.

All of it can result in significant cash outflow to defend the startup business, settle the dispute, or to pay a judgment taken against the Startup Business.

Startup businesses can find themselves legally and financially (and sometimes criminally) responsible for their own management's action or omissions as well as the conduct of those they employ. They may even find themselves legally and/or financially responsible as the result of the defective nature of the products or services they provide.

Each business has its own general risk areas with some very specific risks associated with their particular business, and those risk areas may change from time to time as circumstances evolve.

A well-prepared startup will have a less unpleasant experience with such risks developing, as they will have sought proper advice and implemented management tools to prepare for and deal with such risk in advance. Others will pay big money to catch up and rectify what would have been a relatively minor preventive expense had it been properly addressed and completed earlier.

1. _Managing the Expectations of Founders, Investors, and Shareholders (The "Shotgun Wedding" CAT)_

The relationship between the founders of a startup business is crucial. Too many startups have a great team with energy, talent, and drive, but they fail to take the time to do the "boring stuff", like determining, communicating, and formalizing their roles and expectations of each other and for the business right from the start.

Often, a great creative force needed by the business still wants to retain his or her "day job" because the startup will only be able to pay a living wage later, once it has established itself.

Ambiguity can result on whether that founder/employee is required to contribute as wholeheartedly as the rest, or whether this "absentee" founder is entitled to the same share of the financial rewards of the business. Even worse, this person often ends up in direct competition with the startup, causing increasing stress and conflict.

Often a founder will fail to disclose a fraudulent history, or the fact that he or she has a judgment which places their financial stability and trustworthiness into doubt.

Sometimes people are simply not compatible, and leadership issues arise. Who has the final decision-making power, who has been appointed to that role, and what is the quorum for decision-making? How can a troublesome officer be removed or a deadlock between the founders be resolved? What happens when a founder dies or becomes incapacitated, and the spouse or executor who has no prior experience in the business, needs to step in and make decisions for the business on that person's behalf?

The "shotgun wedding" cat wants to "marry" (in entrepreneur speak this would mean making a heavy commitment in financial or legal terms) as quickly as possible, and who shies away from the things that ought to be discussed in great detail beforehand, even at the risk of provoking the end of the relationship there and then. I am sure you are familiar with the example of someone who got married in haste and avoided finding out that their intended spouse really, really did not want children.

So, take the time to set up a new business, especially when other people are going to be involved, even if they are family. Scrutinize the "mundane" details, ask the awkward questions, and formalize the results and agreements in writing in a unanimous shareholders agreement that specifically deals with your particular business.

CAT#1 Questions/Thoughts To Be Considered:

- What corporate structure to use? How are decision-making (voting powers) and tax strategies to be accommodated in the different share descriptions to be set up in the company?

- What will the ownership (shareholding) be and why? Can this change in the future, and what would be the conditions under which such change may occur?

- Who can decide on changes to shareholding or sale of shares, or even changes to the nature of the business?

- What are the performance expectations of the business relationship and how can they change? How will that affect shareholding?

- What are the long-term goals of the business, and those who own it?

- What are the expectations for payment for services rendered to the business? How are they to be paid?

- What decisions can be made by day-to-day management of the business and what decisions require the involvement of all of the shareholders or directors? How is the quorum defined?

- Who can bind the business to contracts? Who will be able to sign checks on the business bank account? What are the maximum amounts which may be spent in the day-to-day operations of the business and which do not require board approval? How can this be communicated to third parties?

- What checks and balances and accountability systems will be built into the business? How often will management accounts be produced, and who is responsible to get this done?

- What will happen if one of the shareholders or directors die or becomes incapacitated?

- Who will deliver what and for what reward? Some prospective shareholders will provide "sweat equity", some simply bring financial benefits, some have great business contacts and networks, and others will have the required skills and experience to run day-to-day operations. Each of these has a value that is not always easy to compare to the others' offerings.

- Find out the management and working style of your prospects—who is a natural leader and who is the lone operator. Is there a personality issue?

- Ask whether their family is on board with the financial sacrifice needed for the long unpaid hours that most startups require. Is your prospect distracted by unhappy and unsupportive family issues? How much of an impact will this have on the success of the business?

- How will disputes be resolved? What are the exit strategies? What are the prospects' expectations of timelines, payment and return on investment?

- How would the business be valued if a shareholder wants out in the future?

- What skills and experience does your prospect have in startups, similar industries or large corporations?

- What does your personal experience of the prospect tell you (yes—gut feelings matter)?

- Do your due diligence on prospective business associates. Simple searches are available that will reveal if there is a significant debt, bankruptcy or a judgment you should be aware of. Even a simple Google search can raise questions as to the prospect's history and public profile that can impact the success of this business relationship, but always keep in mind the legitimacy of the source of the information.

Lastly, be cautious about giving away a large shareholding in your business to attract talent before you have satisfied yourself that the person can deliver what the business needs. Spend the time and money to set up a carefully drafted formal agreement that allows for a period in which the prospect must prove that he or she can deliver with clear performance parameters, or you will be saddled with a troublesome shareholder who brings less than the business requires and the increased cost of having to bring additional talent to make up the deficiency.

Manage the unknown with thought, anticipate issues that may arise, and spend the time at the very beginning of your business agreements to avoid unnecessary disputes, litigation, and costs in the future.

The time to agree the value of a business or how such value will be determined in the future (and therefore the value of a shareholder's shares) is not on the eve of a significant dispute, when a disgruntled shareholder wants out at the highest possible value, and the remaining shareholders want to pay as little as possible.

2. *The "What Corporate Structure?" CAT*

This cat likes to do things on the cheap, which is why no lawyer was consulted and the company that was incorporated has no foundational management documents, no minute book (what is that anyway?), and most definitely no unanimous shareholders agreement or written contract of any kind. Certainly, it is unlikely that any general security agreement or even promissory note is in place to protect personal funds invested in the business.

Startups generally have little to no cash, so many are incorporated on only the most basic level. Many do not know what a "minute book" might be and why it is needed. The share structure is set up on the most basic of levels, and there is little room for different share categories with different rights and opportunities for differential dividend distribution or restrictions on voting.

Do you even need a corporation? What is the best structure for your particular business? Your lawyer can discuss the various options and explain your personal risk profile in the choice between remaining a "natural person" or incorporating. Accountants often advise against incorporating simply due to the costs involved and the accounting fees attached to the annual financial filings, and the fact that there is little tax advantage in a small startup becoming incorporated. Accountants do not look at managing legal liability risk, and therein lies the rub.

Also, incorporating correctly from the beginning prevents the later cost, complexity, and tax consequences of, for example, rolling over a successful business into a corporate structure and the risk that the tax authority does not accept the rollover. Or the cost and tax implications of changing the share structure once the business is successful and those shares have significant value.

Some businesses are at higher risk levels than others, and the exposure of the decision makers to personal liability need to be managed through a detailed review of the potential risks to the personal assets of the business owners versus the benefits and costs of incorporation.

Partnerships and limited partnerships where more than one person is involved in the business are an option, but are generally not recommended, particularly where the people involved do not know and trust each other really well.

There are many advantages to incorporation other than tax savings, and these can be more fully explored by an experienced and trusted business lawyer with specific focus on your particular business.

Trusts can also be a very useful tool in preserving assets against business risk, particularly if large financial or property contributions will be made for the business.

The wise entrepreneur will also bear in mind that there are many stages of business in which the benefits of incorporation may be interfered with.

In particular, prior to borrowing funds or entering into a lease, consult your lawyer if you are being asked to sign personal guarantees, and determine whether this is necessary. If so, ensure that all involved in the business carry this responsibility equally, at the very least.

CAT#2 Questions/Thoughts To Be Considered:

- How many people will be involved in the business, and how well do they know each other?

- Who will own what percentage of the company and who will control the company?

- What skills, qualifications, experience and talent are represented by those involved in the business? Who will verify, do background checks, call references, perform due diligence and searches?

- Who will make decisions for the various areas of management of the company? Who will be responsible to create, maintain and keep safe records of the company, including financial records?

- What kind of a business will the startup be and who will be its clients? A cake making business run by out of the entrepreneur's home may choose to operate as a sole proprietorship, while a pipeline production business would gain little credibility with its potential clients in the same structure.

- Generally, those business structures that expose the personal assets of those in the business to risk are the unincorporated structures such as sole proprietorships and partnerships and their various forms, which vary from country to country. These are the most nominal form of business enterprise, needing very little formality or annual expenses related to required filings or formal maintenance of corporate structure, and certainly fewer accounting costs. Protection of the name of the personally held business may incur some minor costs in the registration of a trade-name such as in Canada. However, there are significant limits to such protection as discussed in the IP section below.

- All business entities need to be advised of the risks of infringing other business names, particularly trademarks. Many entrepreneurs are not aware of the difference between an incorporated name or a trade-name versus the power of a trademark, and waste much time and branding efforts on a name that cannot be sustained after a challenge.

- What business name should be used (see more on this in the "IP Pirate Cat" section below)?

- What sort of risks surround the business? Do the entrepreneurs in the business have significant personal assets that should be protected against business risk or failure?

- What tax advantages exist for your business? Are there special tax breaks or structures that will allow the splitting of income, passing of dividends, retaining of passive income in the corporation such that you can save for your retirement through the vehicle of your corporation?

3. *The "What Director's Liability?" CAT*

The incorporation of a startup does not absolve the directors of all personal legal liability.

In fact, most jurisdictions place significant personal responsibility for the payment of employees' wages and salaries, and the submission of employee payroll remittances, unemployment insurance and government pension plan contributions upon the directors if the corporation fails to do so.

Decisions made by directors can be subject to "piercing of the corporate veil" in specific circumstances, which will result in personal responsibility for such decisions. Illegal conduct, fraud or tortious conduct whether personally or on behalf of the corporation, can open the door to personal liability.

Once a startup is ready for public funding, or even where private investors are coming aboard, a director is expected to be well informed of the facts and the financial situation of the company and take care not to mislead such investors.

Errors and omissions liability insurance is advisable, but may not cover every instance where a director may be called to personally make good the actions of a corporation.

Directors are duty bound to act in good faith and honestly in the best interests of the corporation and to avoid and disclose any conflicts of interest between their personal affairs and those of the company. Directors also owe a duty of care to act in the interests of the corporation as carefully, diligently and skillfully as a prudent person would in similar circumstances. Each director is expected to apply specialized skills to the benefit of the corporation should they possess such skills.

Becoming a director or officer of a corporation is no light undertaking—seek the advice of an experienced lawyer to get an understanding of your responsibilities and have that lawyer on call for the day-to-day business events that require careful analysis of your personal exposure.

4. *The "Contract on a Napkin" CAT*

Most businesses know the terms on which they need to do business successfully. They understand the need to make a profit from their operations and to keep their administration smooth, predictable and free of unnecessary complexity. Customers, employees and suppliers should be given consistent and clear terms to keep administrative costs and expectations under control and reduce the opportunity for disputes.

Yet, so many businesses do a quote on a napkin or contract orally and then wonder why there has been a misunderstanding as to the final price, expectation of delivery, or failure to meet the required standards of their client resulting in resistance to payment, upset subcontractors who want their money, and all the other "joys" which can visit business owners who didn't prepare properly.

Still, more do not know the basic consumer protections provided by legislation which causes unnecessary delays in resolving disputes, which then escalate to costly litigation.

It is so worth it to have a set of standard contracts drawn up by a competent lawyer who knows your business and its specific risk areas.

Some things don't fit on a napkin, but are vitally important to outline in writing before commencing a new business relationship whether employment, supply contract or customer work.

CAT#4 Questions/Thoughts To Consider:

- Who are the contracting parties (wow, if I had a dollar for each time this is done poorly AND for the amount of time that sole shareholders carelessly confuse their own identity with that of their corporation thereby putting themselves on the line personally).

- Certainty as to the deliverables, their quality, time and place of delivery, passing of risk for damage to delivered products.

- The substantive law which governs the contract, and where (and sometimes in which language) will the dispute be heard? Who will decide which of the parties was right all along—a public court, or a private arbitration (how much do you want your business dealings to be made public?).

- Performance measures and clear expectations—when is it clear that the contract has not been not properly performed.

- How to get out of dodge—when the contract and the relationship goes sour.

- Breach, termination and dispute resolution clauses.

- Clarity on the compensation, delivery method and costs, and whether GST or other sales taxes are included or excluded.

- Clarity on the term and duration of the contract, renewal clauses and whether any obligations survive the end of the contract.

- Protection for intellectual property, clarity on ownership of developed IP through a joint venture or employment.

- Confidentiality, non-compete, non-solicitation considerations.

- Limitation of liability, particularly for consequential damages.

- Force major and other no-fault breach provisions.

If you do business over the internet, these standard contracts can and should be adapted for such use and incorporated into your website. Your clients must click to accept the contractual terms before they can do business on the internet with you.

5. *The "Privacy and Social Media Is So "New Age"" CAT*

This is only true if you've been hiding under a rock for the past ten years. There have been significant advances in privacy laws in recent years, and they are being enforced more and more. At the very least, startups need to have a publicly accessible privacy policy, address the privacy issues surrounding the gathering of client information, the reasons they are doing such collecting, the care they must take to ensure such private information remains private while on their servers or in their possession. They also need a privacy officer to deal with complaints.

In addition, to be a successful business in the digital age, startups need to have a social media and internet presence, and that comes with its own legal liability challenges.

As a business startup you will be advised by marketing gurus that email marketing and that all elusive marketing list is the key to success. That may well be, but they fail to advise you on the incredibly heavy penalties that some jurisdictions are imposing for unsolicited business emails, and how falling foul of these rules can end the life of your startup in a few "easy" emails.

Legislation such as the Canadian Anti-Spam Legislation (CASL) have massive financial penalties for failing to manage, document and maintain your email permissions carefully.

Social media is very tempting but also must be carefully managed to avoid liability for false advertising, misrepresentations, defamation claims, privacy concerns, intellectual property infringements and poor choices generally. Employees and marketing gurus who do the postings should be given clear guidelines and a social media policy should be in place both for private use by an employee or when representing the corporation.

It is important to note the fact that social media and internet marketing is international (and thereby also subject to international laws), instant and easily repeatable. It is subject to "whatever happens on the internet stays on the internet" longevity and can also be hacked.

6. *The "IP Pirate" CAT*

IP, or intellectual property, is a concept many startups are aware of but very often do not fully understand, mainly because they do not practice preventive law to consult with their lawyer ahead of time. They do not get a full picture of its intrinsic value and the increasing seriousness with which other business owners are now enforcing their rights.

This area of legal liability is exceptionally wide and touches many areas of the "fun stuff" in a startup's early days—the glamour of coming up with a funky business name, a fantastic logo and loads of brand centered, colorful marketing materials upon which they are told, the fate of a growing business depends.

The problem is that the "fun stuff" takes over the previously rational mind of the startup founders, and soon they lose all sense chasing pretty colors, glossy designs and cool marketing gimmicks. They pay a fortune to the marketing gurus and then launch to massive fanfare, only to get a nasty enthusiasm killing cease and desist letter in the mail the following week.

CAT#6 Questions/Thoughts To Be Considered:

- What name, colors, and logo do you want to use for your business? Make it unique to avoid the trademark debacle later in the life of the business.

- Do a domain name and trademark search, not just a basic pre-incorporation name search. Search your name *and* logo (Cadbury have actually protected the particular shade of purple used on their bars, believe it or not!).

- Ensure that your marketing gurus have the experience and integrity to design your marketing material from scratch, and have them bound to a solid contract that holds them accountable for copyright and other intellectual property infringement actions or claims. Do not simply sign off on *their* standard form contract that very likely absolves them of all responsibility. I recall a case wherein a graphic artist allegedly used a copy of an international proprietary microphone design to make up the foundation of a logo for a local music company, which needless to say, became a potential international IP lawsuit and wasted significant amounts of the client's cash.

- Understand the difference in IP protection offered by a trade-name, a corporate name and a specific country trademark or one that is registered in several countries. Understand the interaction between the various trademark arrangements internationally, and how your lovingly and expensively developed local brand can be challenged in the future without trademark protection.

- If you intend to spread your wings internationally, then also do a trademark search in the countries you intend to get into and start the registration process.

- Who owns your IP? This is an important consideration to keep in mind in the heady days of "free stuff" being thrown about. After all, who has time to read the "fine print" of that free website designer that you just commissioned to produce and host your website, upon which all your organic reach is going to be built?

- If your startup business in in the creative field in any respect whatsoever, then you need to be clear with contractors and employees as to the ownership of the IP in materials, concepts or designs, copyright, trademarks, patents or inventions, business processes, computer programs, or any other form of IP created both while they are at work or even at home (if you're being really thorough).

- Make sure your own products or services do not infringe copyright or other intellectual property rights of others and take steps to formalize any previously tolerated or verbally permitted use of third-party IP before it becomes an issue.

- Watch your website for copyright infringement by other businesses. This happens a LOT and is a backhanded "compliment" that can confuse your clients and hurt your reputation.

7. *The "Tax and Regulation Dodger" CAT*

Every business exists for the purpose of paying a tax, as many governments might say.

Do not sink your startup ship for failure to make your tax collector happy. This is one sure way to fail in those first five years.

Get your startup registered and submit the paperwork for income tax, sales tax, remittances, and all licenses, permits, property and business taxes and every other government mandated draw on your hard-earned money as soon as possible. Keep meticulous records and submit your fees on an ongoing basis.

Get specific local legal advice on these matters as a priority.

8. *The "Employment Laws Are for Sissies" CAT*

Becoming an employer is yet another milestone in the maturing business owner's list of satisfactions and achievements. Congratulations, you are now responsible for the support of your employee and his or her family. Government regulations take this very seriously.

Employees remittances, annual income earnings statements, record of employment, calculations of deductions for income tax, remittances for employment insurance, government mandated pensions, workmen's compensation and so on must be done at every pay period.

Falling behind and failing to submit regular reports and payments will again sink your startup ship in no time at all. Plus, you'll have a very powerful and sometimes nasty creditor to deal with. No point in making all those phishing scam calls about your going to jail for debts owed to the Canadian Revenue Agency (or your particular tax collector) come true.

Make sure you know the difference between an employee and an independent contractor, and make sure that your friendly tax collector agrees with your assessment. It is not what *you* name your contract, it is what the tax collector deems it to be.

Once again, an employment contract is important for fairness and clarity of the terms of service, management of expectations, codes of conduct, and can mean a huge saving in money and potential litigation.

Letting go of an employee is never easy, and there is significant risk in doing so. Having that great relationship with a lawyer well-versed in your business, and whom you like and trust, can save you premature aging.

Ensure that you know the law with respect to hours worked, overtime, vacation entitlement, maternity and other family or compassionate leave and all other requirements for your specific jurisdiction.

Time and money invested in an employment contract where employee performance expectations, IP issues, pay expectations, bonus provisions and retention incentives are clearly spelled out can mean the difference between a happy and motivated employee versus one who sues your startup and files complaint with the authorities.

Harassment will be a major focus in business going forward, and responsibility falls on the startup owner to ensure proper conduct expectations and reporting procedures are in place to deal with these high-risk issues, ideally prior to an incident arising.

Time spent on thinking through all areas of concern relative to the employment situation in your particular business will save significant time and costs in the future.

CAT#8 Questions/Thoughts To Consider:

- Make sure you check your employee's references, background and police checks. Make it clear that the latter will be done on an ongoing basis and may result in termination if not satisfactory, particularly if your business deals with vulnerable people as clients such as youth or the elderly.

- Make sure the employee is the right "fit" first.

- Prepare a written employment contract. This goes for startup founders who are expected to work in the business, too.

- Clarify whether the employee is in fact an employee or an independent contractor.

- Expected hours of work, including whether overtime is required. Think about and complete a clear and reasonably broad ranging job description.

- Remuneration, bonus expectations, other employee retention incentives such as stock options, share performance units.

- Probationary periods are gold—use them!

- Duration of the contract.

- Termination, confidentiality, non-solicitation and non-compete provisions (must be reasonable).

- IP ownership and assignment.

- An employee handbook and/or code of conduct.

In Conclusion

The above discussion is meant as a starting point for entrepreneurs to begin to understand and think about the many issues they need to get "right" while also trying to market and grow their businesses. You should acknowledge that you need to be fairly superhuman if you insist on going it alone.

Entrepreneurs live a singularly challenging life—long hours at work while others relax at home and enjoy family time. There is much sacrifice and a reasonable reward would be well earned.

There is no reason to risk that reward by failing to obtain good, practical advice at the time you need it most, so I leave you with the following considerations of how to find that perfect legal eagle to fly alongside your growing startup and help reach its much-deserved success.

Look for a lawyer through referrals from friends and business colleagues or the law society in your area, and interview several different ones until you find one:

- **With experience** in several areas of business law — not just in law, but in life.

- **Who is competent,** practical and professional.

- **Who gives you confidence** that they have thought their advice through, not empty promises.

- **With a sense of humor** – the law can be horribly boring stuff to go through without it.

- **Who is courageous** and not reticent about confronting opposing counsel where necessary and in your best interests, or bringing an appeal where a challenge to a judgment may be appropriate.

- **Who answers your calls** – fire those who leave you hanging for weeks, whatever their reputation. They're just not that into you or your business.

- **Whose advice you understand** – someone you feel comfortable asking questions of and who engages with you instead of "lecturing". No question should make you feel inadequate – this is not an intelligence competition - but always keep in mind the legitimacy of the source of the information.

- **Who carefully listens to your story** and is genuinely interested in your business and its challenges.

- **Who has a passion for small business** and really wants to help and see you succeed.

- **Who is honest and transparent** and will give you bad news if you need to hear it, thereby saving you unnecessary legal fees fighting a losing battle, so you can settle instead

- **Who favors preventive law and staying out of court,** but who can strongly back you up with litigation experience if necessary.

Also remember that a good lawyer is always busy and in demand – that is the nature of their business, and that if you anticipate needing help on a new project or problem, consider providing reasonable notice whenever possible to keep the relationship sweet. Also, chocolate and wine are always welcome—we love being recognized for keeping you out of trouble!

**Download ten legal issues
for startup business owners to manage:
www.skajalaw.ca/5YearBizGuide**

*Manage the unknown with thought, anticipate
issues that may arise, and spend the time at the very
beginning of your business agreements to avoid
unnecessary disputes, litigation, and costs in the future.*

*This is not an easy journey. It requires dedication,
resilience, and a lot of really hard work.*

CHAPTER 11

STAYING AT THE TOP OF YOUR GAME

Reaching the 5-year milestone is what business owners strive for. You wait for the day when you have gone through the growing pains and are finally profitable. You may be dreaming of the day that you can take a vacation and still be making money.

This is not an easy journey. It requires dedication, resilience, and a lot of really hard work.

When you first start out, things will be pretty lean. As a solopreneur, it's difficult to stay optimistic, motivated, and focused at all times (and we've all been there, so you're not alone).

It's a matter of finding a way for you to continually stay on top of your game. You are the visionary, builder, and cheerleader all in one. And while this can be a lonely journey at times, the positives outweigh the negatives for so many business owners.

The key to owning and running a successful business is to surround yourself with people that can help pick you up every time you fall.

There will be days when you may wonder, *what did I get myself into?*

You will be pounding the pavement, and all you will hear at times is, "No thank you."

You may feel like you are beating your head against a wall. It's a matter of being strong and perhaps leaving sticky notes in your office to remind yourself that yes, in fact, "You can do it!"

Your mindset and attitude are what will keep you going.

Thomas Edison once said, "I have not failed. I've just found 10,000 ways that won't work."

As you map your journey, you will realize that the road is not always direct or straight. There will be the expected stop lights and turns, and you will also run into construction zones where there may be delays or detours. You must plan for it and be flexible to adapt to the changing conditions.

There will be times where you know what the logical next step is, and it is definitely outside of your comfort zone. Perhaps it's speaking in front of a group of 100 people or writing a book. For personal growth, you need to push through your fears and take that leap forward. There will be lots of people behind you rooting for you.

After it is done, you will get a rush of energy when you realize, *that wasn't so bad*. Or you will say, "I just found another way that won't work!" and you will be one step closer to finding the one that will work.

When you have wins, celebrate them, no matter how small they are. Find yourself a cheerleading team that will encourage you and say, "Way to go!"

Sometimes it's posting your wins on social media or going out for a drink to celebrate. You will find that this will give you a burst of energy to keep going to take the next step.

Procrastination is rampant among business owners, especially for those who work from home. It's really easy to say, "I'll do it after the dishes are done," or sleep in for an extra hour or two because you can.

This is where the discipline comes in. Perhaps it's having your home office separate from your living space, or setting up office hours to separate personal tasks from working on your business. Over time, you will realize that you have created a routine that works best for you. If you track your time, make sure you are putting in at least forty hours per week on your business.

There are many distractions that can get in the way when you work from home. If you are having problems staying focused, try one of these ideas. Not all will work for everyone. It's a matter of finding out what is most effective for you:

- **Top three goals for the week** – At the beginning of the week, write down three activities you want to complete that will help move your business forward.

- **Take frequent breaks to refresh your energy level** – Set a timer where every hour you get up from your computer to go for a five-minute walk, meditate, or just crank up the music and dance!

- **Find an accountability partner** – They don't need to have a ton of business experience, they just have to be someone who will hold you accountable for your commitments. Everyday, text or email your partner to say what your one intention is for the day. The next day, text or email to say whether you completed the task and what your intention is for the new day. This is two-sided, so you are helping each other be accountable.

- **Schedule important or repetitive tasks into your calendar** – You can decide that every Saturday at 1 pm is when you do your bookkeeping and pay your bills. This helps from getting distracted during the week. You can also block off specific days of the week to be your "catch up" days. If it's in your calendar, you will have a better chance of doing it.

- **Turn off your most common distractions** – You might want to turn off your personal email or social media during business hours so that annoying beep doesn't come up when a new message is received.

Many people have a weakness for TV—whether it's the old-fashioned box or watching online movies or shows. Consider using TV as a reward for when you have achieved your designated task for the day.

> *Thomas Edison once said, "I have not failed. I've just found 10,000 ways that won't work."*

Self-care

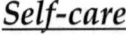

You cannot take care of your clients and your business if you are not taking care of yourself. It is important that you are in peak form, happy, and fully recharged to give your clients the attention they need and deserve. Sick time can greatly impact your business and your income, especially if you are in the startup phase.

Here are some general tips I practice myself:

- **Schedule in exercise time** – Whether it's going for walks or to the gym, choose something you enjoy that will give you energy and keep you healthy.

- **Eat nutritious meals** – Know what foods give you energy and what drains you.

- **Get a good night sleep** – You will make more mistakes if you are constantly tired.

- **Drink lots of water** – You will be able to think clearer when your brain is hydrated.

- **Meditate** – This clears the mind and allows you to be more creative with your ideas. CEO's of large organizations have been known to start their day meditating.

- **Create a bright, positive work space** – One that will lift your energy and make you want to go to work in the morning. Some people incorporate Feng Shui techniques to create this environment.

- **Incorporate ergonomic practices around your computer** – This includes having your monitors and keyboard/mouse at the right heights and a chair with proper support. This will prevent back, neck, and wrist pain.

If you seem to be constantly stressed, track what you are doing during these times of worry. Identifying your stressors means you can now find a solution for them.

Being overwhelmed is one of the bigger stressors. Breaking things down into manageable pieces may make a big difference. Some people have a problem breaking things down. In these situations, it's easier to work with an accountability coach. Sometimes it's approaching the situation from a different perspective that makes a difference. My clients have found it very helpful to have me, as an outsider, break things down for them.

Sometimes there are people who are continually not achieving their tasks. The same to-do items keep showing up on the weekly list, and they are just not getting done. This is a sign that there may be a blockage somewhere. It could be something deep in the back of your mind from the past that is holding you back from moving forward.

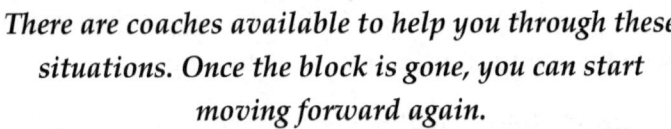

There are coaches available to help you through these situations. Once the block is gone, you can start moving forward again.

The Power of Collaboration

The road to building a business can be a lonely one. No one is expected to know or do everything. It's simply not practical.

In a large corporation, if the company decided to develop a new product, one of the first things that would happen would be the executive management team getting together for a meeting. This meeting would normally consist of the president, vice president of sales, operations manager, chief financial officer (CFO), and the information technology (IT) person.

The president may have a vision and present it at the meeting. The operations manager may say that this new direction would require more personnel and operational changes. The information technology person may say that if there are more people, then new systems will need to be purchased to accommodate the growth. The VP sales may suggest a whole new marketing strategy. Then the CFO will ask where the money is coming from and then realize that they will figure it out and make it happen. This is a *team* effort.

As a startup business, you may not have the experience to understand how all the pieces that go together. This is why you would need to get some outside help to guide you so the pieces come together faster.

There are many specialists out there that can help you with the individual components for your business. They will give you their perspective based on their area of expertise. Ideally, you should find someone who has experience in all these areas and can take a holistic approach to your business. Once you know what the whole picture looks like, you can then get help from the individual specialists.

It's like putting together a puzzle. If you have a bunch of puzzle pieces and no picture, it will take much longer to finish. With someone who takes a holistic approach with the business, they can show you what the puzzle looks like first before hiring the specialists to build it.

What you don't want to do is to play whack-a-mole with your business, where you fix one problem and have another problem pop up as a result of the first one. If you put in a huge marketing campaign to bring in lots of new clients, and you don't have the capacity to handle the additional volume of business, you run the risk of having unhappy customers and running yourself to the ground.

Instead of being reactive in your business, having the right person to help you allows you to be proactive to anticipate problems before they happen. Paying for the help up front can save you time and money in the long run and allows you to reach your goals faster.

As with the athlete, they will have different coaches through different stages of their training. They may also have different types of coaches working with them from a performance coach to nutrition and mindset.

Take the best from all and learn your lessons.

Bottom line is that, for your business, you may have different people helping you out at different stages. They will each have different areas of specialty and bring different perspectives. Whether you call it a coach, consultant, strategist, mentor or advisor, you should find one that is the best fit for you and your business at this time.

Here are some tips on choosing who to work with:

- **Skill set** – Is their area of expertise what you need for your business at this time?

- **Experience** – How much hands-on business experience do they have? Sometimes having a person who has experience from a different industry can be an advantage, as they may be able to have a unique view on your business.

- **Service deliverable** – Are they offering what you need for your business—group coaching, training, one-on-one, etc.

- **Personality and style** – Do you have a connection with this person? Do they have a style that works for you?

If you are not sure whether the person is a right fit for you and your business, then perhaps engage them in one of their smaller services to test it out before making a larger commitment.

Instead of paying for someone to guide your business, you can create a small group of your peers and become a support group for each other. This is a great way of brainstorming new ways of doing things and testing new ideas. One thing to keep in mind is that when you bring a problem to the group, they are answering the question based on the information you supply them. They might not be aware of the entire situation and the missing piece of information could impact the results.

If someone asks, "Should I be on Twitter?", your group might share their own personal experiences with Twitter. In reality, they might not know that your target market is business professionals, and LinkedIn might be a better social media platform for you to market your services.

As business owners, we naturally want to help each other out. The reality is everyone has a business to run and helping you run yours is probably not their top priority.

The key to successful collaboration is to listen to all ideas and be open-minded. Sometimes the most obscure suggestions can trigger something else that becomes a great idea. Everyone has experienced variant things in their life, so they will always offer a distinct perspective rather than your own.

Sometimes we are too close to the situation that we don't see the obvious answers in front of us. Or you might be too emotionally attached to see things objectively. Or you have never come across a situation like that before. The true power of collaboration is opening your eyes to see things you cannot see and learning from each other.

The journey for a business owner can be a lonely road. However, you can achieve your dreams faster if you surround yourself with people who are positive influences for you. There will be many people who will come and go on your journey, and you will learn from all. Take the best from all and learn your lessons.

Now that you have the road map for the first five years…it's time to drive.

Bon voyage and enjoy the journey!

LET'S GET STARTED!

Here are some Canadian resources to help you get started.

NCP Consulting Services

Helping overwhelmed business owners get
clarity, direction and results
www.NCPConsulting.net
Nicki Chang-Powless - Nicki@NCPConsulting.net

HotSpot Social Media (Chapter 6)

Effortless social media for small businesses
www.hotspotsocialmedia.com
Darlene Hull - Darlene@hotspotsocialmedia.com

Skaja Law (Chapter 10)

Powerful Personal Representation
www.skajalaw.ca
Marion Skaja - marion.skaja@skajalaw.com

Advance Insurance Educational Services Inc. (Page 33)

Protecting your personal and business assets
www.aieacademy.ca
Helene Wood - helene@aieacademy.ca

CFO to Go Canada (Page 113)
Your CFO while you GROW
www.cfo2gocanada.com
Todd Purcell – todd@cfo2gocanada.com or
todd@albertabusinessloans.com

Follow It Thru Publishing (Page 76)
Helping bring your story to life in a novel way with impact and influence
www.Heatherandrews.press www.followitthrupublishing.com
Heather Andrews – heather@followitthru.com

High Power Solutions Accounting (Page 128)
Helping small business owners sleep better by taking away the money stress.
www.highpowersolutions.ca
Tina Saini - Tina@HighPowerSolutions.ca

KIS Payments (Page 27)
Accepting Credit Card Payments – Simple Service and Solutions
www.kispayments.com
Jennifer Belik – jenn@kispayments.com

Little Blue Bug Studios (Page 73)

Creating a brand is more than just graphics, it's raising the bar. When you define your brand, you up-level your business!

www.bluebugstudios.com

Lorraine Shulba – hello@lshulba.com

The Networking Web (Page 81)

Generating sales with simplified digital marketing strategies

www.thenetworkingweb.com

Catherine Saykaly-Stevens - Catherine@thenetworkingweb.com

DOWNLOAD RESOURCES
FROM THE EXPERTS

www.NCPConsulting.net/5YearBizGuide
Business road map template for a startup business

www.hotspotsocialmedia.com/5YearBizGuide
10 days to a Simple, Step-by-Step, Social Media System for Small Businesses and a 30-minute strategy session to help you put it together!

www.skajalaw.ca/5YearBizGuide
10 legal issues for startup business owners to manage

www.aieacademy.ca/5YearBizGuide
List of things to bring when getting commercial insurance

www.cfo2gocanada.com/5YearBizGuide
What to put into your business plan for the bank

www.followitthru.com/5YearBizGuide
The top ten things to consider when publishing

www.highpowersolutions.ca/5YearBizGuide
Interview questions when hiring bookkeeper and accountant

www.highpowersolutions.ca/5YearBizGuide
Calculate how much money you need to save for retirement to maintain current lifestyle

www.kispayments.com/5YearBizGuide
Considerations when selecting credit card processing provider

www.bluebugstudios.com/5YearBizGuide
5 things to consider when branding your business

www.thenetworkingweb.com/5YearBizGuide
A digital marketing campaign example - broken down into simple steps

ABOUT THE AUTHOR

Nicki Chang-Powless, B.Sc.Eng is an award-winning entrepreneur, author, speaker, educator, consultant, and business strategist. Her passion is to help improve the number of businesses that succeed past those critical first five years.

Nicki is a strong believer that it takes the diversity of a team to build a business. Her philosophy is based on "NetCP – Network, Collaborate and Profit". You can achieve success on your own, but you can get there much faster if you have a strong team behind you.

All of Nicki's programs are based on RADAR - her five-step system that will help navigate businesses and keep them on track.

Review – Where are you now, and where do you want to go?

Analyze – Look at all your options and analyze the situation to determine which ones are best for you.

Develop a plan – Based on your options, create a roadmap that is easy for you to follow.

Action – With the roadmap, it's time to take action. It doesn't happen on its own!

Reassess – On every journey, there will be speed bumps, detours and construction zones. Continually evaluate the situation to make sure you stay on course.

Outside of business, Nicki is a fine art and concert photographer. Many of her images have won awards at local camera clubs, including Image of the Year. She has travelled five continents with her husband photographing the landscape, culture, and wildlife. Her adventures included visiting polar bears in Churchill, Manitoba, and penguins in Antarctica. The highlight of her photography career was being an accredited photographer at the 2016 JUNO Canadian Music Awards. Nicki incorporates her photography into her consulting business from her social media posts to her products like journals and her 12 Months of Inspiration calendar.

Nicki lives in Calgary, Alberta, Canada with her husband of over twenty-five years, while her two children have left home to create a life of their own.

Connect with Nicki Chang-Powless at Nicki@NCPConsulting.net

Website - www.NCPConsulting.net

Facebook - facebook.com/nicki.changpowless

LinkedIn - linkedin.com/in/nickicp/

Programs from Nicki Chang-Powless and NCP Consulting Services

NCP CONSULTING SERVICES
Building Strategies for Success!

Kickstart Program

Take your business to the next level with a simple easy-to-follow road map. From defining your target market and creating an engaging marketing message, to product pricing and marketing strategies, this one-on-one program will give you clarity and direction for your business. Work smarter, not harder.

> *"... (Nicki) has changed our lives! We were at the point that we felt like we were spinning our wheels, but after working with Nicki we now feel more focused and a whole lot less stressed!"*

> – Keltie Masters, Back to Nature Retreat

Magic in the Numbers

Bring more profit to your business by getting to know your numbers. Discover how to take both your accounting and production numbers and make it work for you. Get a complete financial picture of your business.

> *"The way the material is presented and explained helps a person make sense of it all and understand its importance!"*

> – Helene Wood, Advance Insurance Education Inc.

Pitch Perfect Collaborative Workshop

STAND OUT from the crowd with a head turning marketing message designed to catch attention and shorten your sales cycle. Get feedback from your peers on how to make your message better and get ideas for potential new target markets.

"Nicki's Pitch Perfect Workshop gives great tools to anyone who needs to get a clear, simple pitch for your business. I enjoyed its sharing in the group when we did our own pitch. Very helpful!"

– Muriel Skog, Décor Stylist, For Starters Inc.

Marketing Madness Collaborative Workshop

Find out where your perfect prospects are hiding without breaking the bank. Time is precious so focus on getting the biggest bang for your buck. Brainstorm new ideas in a collaborative setting. Leave with new ideas on how to reach your target audience.

"Nicki provides an informative, safe environment to discuss marketing needs. I took away excellent, valuable information."

– Shelly Priest, Photographer, Eclectic Shots

Successful Sales Strategies Collaborative Workshop

Discover how to get more customers to say "YES" faster and more often! These simple techniques will leave you feeling more confident and a new outlook on how to successfully make each prospect count!

"Nicki's knowledge and presentation are excellent. The information is well organized and clearly reflects the strength of her business background. She has been in the trenches and know what she is talking about."

– Donna Neumann, Annie & FREDERICK Inc.

CPSIA information can be obtained
at www.ICGtesting.com
Printed in the USA
LVHW050838061118
595976LV00008B/526